SEW CUTE TO CARRY

12 stylish bag patterns for handbags, purses & totes

D&C
David and Charles

www.stitchcraftcreate.co.uk

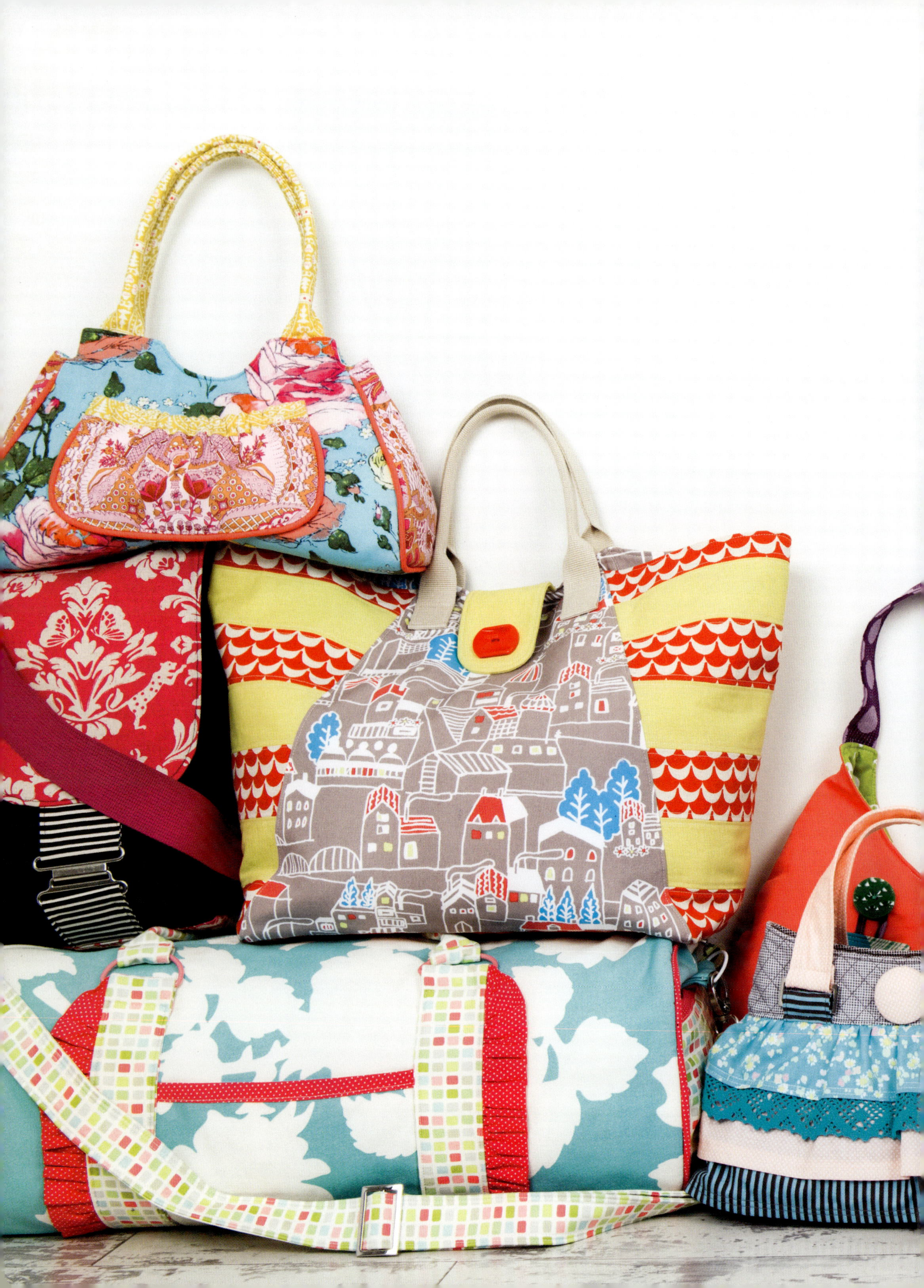

SEW CUTE TO CARRY

Melanie McNeice

CONTENTS

HELLO! 6

TOOLS & MATERIALS 8

Sew Cute Bags 16

Beautiful Blooms Handbag 18

City Nights Clutch 24

Cute Carry-All 30

Blue Skies Backpack 38

Melly's Messenger 46

Happy Hobo Bag 54

Mobile Mummy Changing Bag 60

Shopaholic's Shopper 68

Sugar Sweet Shoulder Bag 74

Wine and Dine Duo 82

Luscious Layered Bag 90

Ruffle Duffle 98

TECHNIQUES.................108

SUPPLIERS..................124

THANK YOU!.................125

THE AUTHOR.................126

INDEX......................127

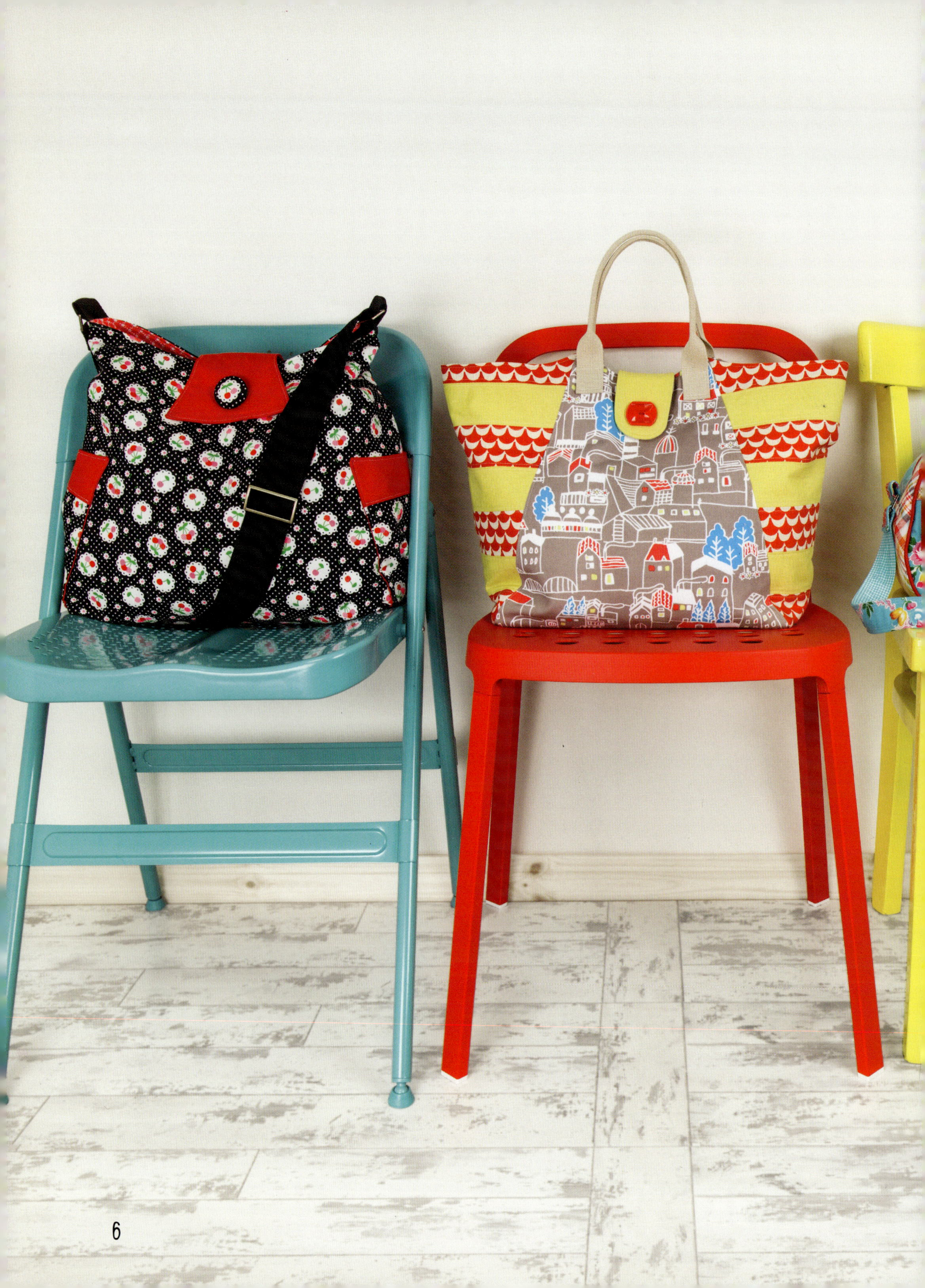

HELLO!

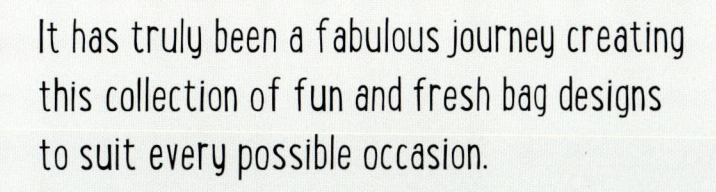

It has truly been a fabulous journey creating this collection of fun and fresh bag designs to suit every possible occasion.

My first original design in 2006 was a handbag. Since that initial project I have developed a passion for creating new bag shapes using interesting fabric combinations. Bag making has been the 'first love' along my sewing journey.

So what a pleasure it is to now introduce you to this collection of twelve unique bag designs, from clutches to changing bags, shoulder bags to shoppers. You will find projects to suit every skill level, from intermediate to more practised sewers: the skill level is clearly indicated by the number of 👜 icons displayed at the start of each pattern (one for beginners, five for advanced sewers). I have included full-size templates for each of the projects, which can be found in the Pattern Pullout Sheet at the back of the book.

If you are patient and feel ready for a challenge then I like to think that whatever your skill level you can tackle most of the bags in this book. Do not be put off or scared by new techniques, as they are often a lot easier than you would ever imagine and can open up a whole new world of bag making possibilities. In the techniques section you will find more detailed explanations of many of the skills used – I hope these will make you feel more confident and ready to tackle that new favourite bag!

Melly x

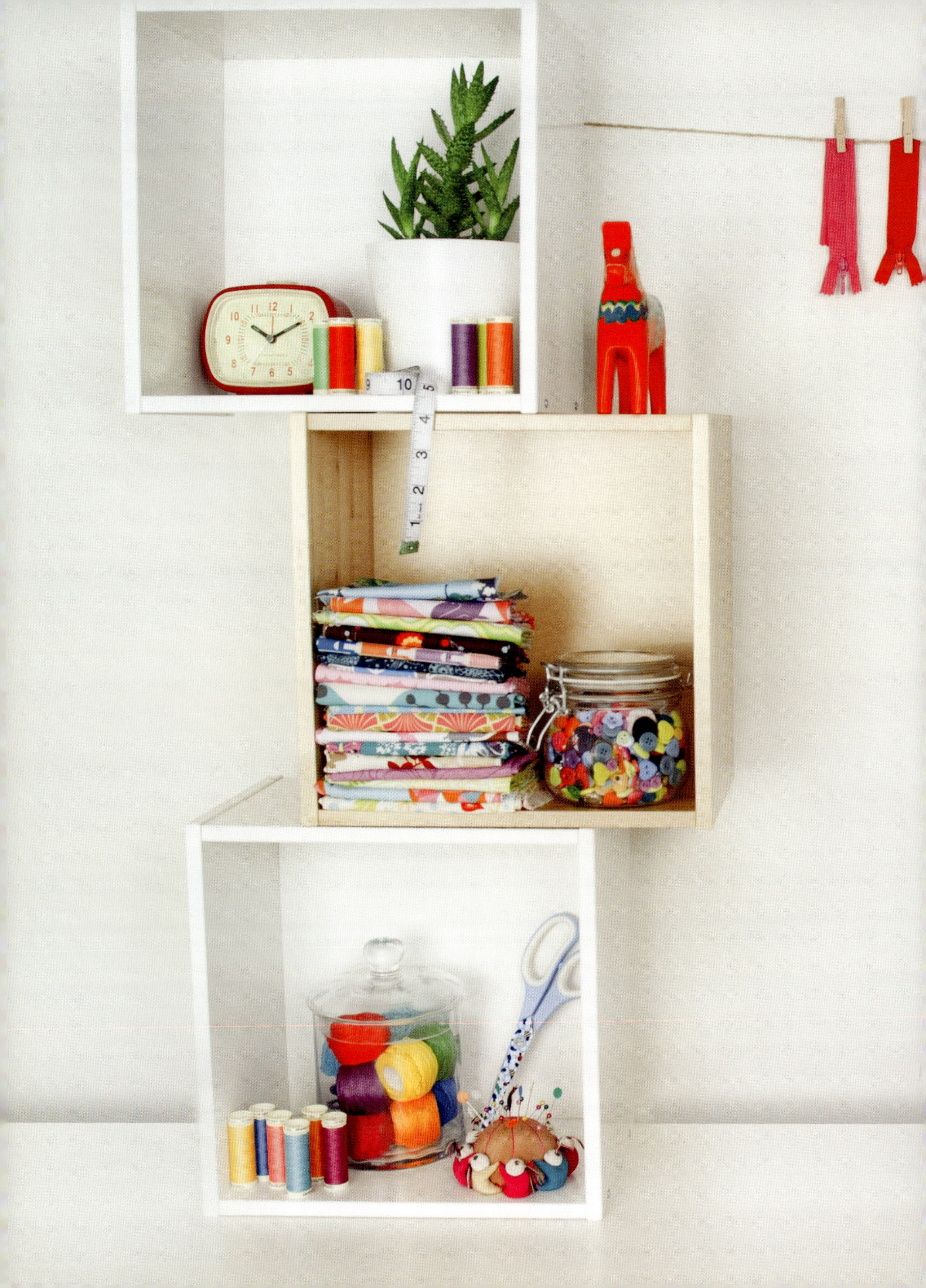

TOOLS
& MATERIALS

TOOLS & MATERIALS

Basic Sewing Tool Kit

Make sure you have the following items to hand before you embark on making any of the bags in this book. All the essentials specified here should be a part of your basic sewing tool kit:

1. TRACING PAPER OR TEMPLATE PLASTIC

These are the best tools to use for tracing your bag patterns (see Pattern Pullout Sheet). I recommend these products in particular because you can clearly see your fabrics through them, making correct placement easier. The markings on the patterns can easily be transferred onto tracing paper or template plastic using a pencil or permanent marker.

2. FABRIC MARKERS

There are many different methods of marking your fabric and you will find an array of products on the market for this purpose. However, vanishing markers or tailor's chalk are the best options in order to avoid making permanent marks on your bags. A light grey lead pencil is a handy substitute.

3. ROTARY CUTTER, MAT AND RULER

These tools are designed to make the cutting of strips and squares a simple and accurate procedure. Although highly recommended, they are not essential items and you can use a tape measure, ruler and scissors instead.

4. SEWING SCISSORS

These are frequently used when sewing any fabric project. I strongly recommend that you invest in good quality scissors to make your sewing experience more accurate and pleasurable. A quality pair of scissors in a large and small size will cover everything from cutting out your fabrics to snipping seams and threads.

5. SEWING THREAD

It is up to you as to your preference for using cotton or polyester thread. I often work with polyester thread when sewing bags as I find that it gives added strength and durability. Have thread available in a few colours to allow for different coloured fabric – sometimes you may like to create a contrast with your stitching, but you will mostly want the thread to tone in with your project. Always have a neutral, black and red spool of thread on hand as a minimum.

6. SEWING MACHINE NEEDLES

Throughout the projects you will be sewing fabrics with varying degrees of thickness. Some materials will have a great deal of bulk, therefore you will need a good range of universal needles in sizes 70, 80, 90 and 100. Many people neglect to change needle sizes as a result they then have great difficulty in getting their machine to sew efficiently through a thick material and even experience tension issues. Always change needles as you work; for some projects you may need to swap needles several times.

7. HAND SEWING NEEDLE

There is a small amount of hand sewing involved in making bags and it is therefore necessary to have a good hand sewing needle. I use and recommend a good quality size 10 embroidery needle for any hand sewing.

①
②
③
④
⑤
⑥
⑦

TOOLS & MATERIALS

Bag Making Tools and Materials

In this book I make reference to different materials, notions and hardware. I recommend that you plan for your bag making before the day you plan to sew. Interesting fabric, notions and hardware can make such a difference to your end result, so it is worth finding nice products to work with. Sometimes hardware can be difficult to track down at your local shops, so try searching online; you will be surprised how many lovely items can be found at home and overseas to add that professional wow factor to your work.

MATERIALS & NOTIONS

1. FABRIC

I have only used 100% cotton fabrics and make reference to patchwork fabric and home décor weight fabric. I like to use home décor weight (medium/heavy weight) fabric for most bags over a certain size. I find that the extra weight in the fabric makes a much stronger, more structured bag that is hardwearing and will hold the correct shape. You can substitute home décor weight fabrics for standard patchwork fabrics, but be aware that your end result will differ.

2. FUSIBLE FLEECE/INTERFACING

In all of my projects I refer to lightweight fusible fleece – a white, lightweight interfacing that is often used in bag construction. It has a fusible glue surface on one side, and gives a thicker, softer structure. I prefer to use a lightweight fleece and then use it on both the main bag and the lining so that they both have adequate strength and structure. However, you can use a thicker fleece if you like, and omit interfacing the lining. I also may make reference to other interfacings, which will be standard dressmaking interfacing.

3. WEBBING

Webbing is a great product that can be used to create tough bag handles quickly. It is available in natural and synthetic fibres through some sewing supply shops, as well as online. Some patchwork fabric companies are starting to add webbing to their range of products.

4. CORD

Cotton cord is used to make piping or as a pull string. When being used for piping on a bag, use cord that is approximately 3–4mm (⅛in) in diameter. If you are using a dark fabric for your piping, try to find a dark coloured cord to ensure there is no show through.

5. SELF-COVER BUTTONS

A great range of self-cover buttons is available on the market in a large variety of sizes. I love to use these buttons to add a professional touch to my bag designs. You can use any type of self-cover buttons; simply follow the instructions on the packet to make them. Experiment by cutting out a fabric element you really want to make a feature of.

6. PRE-MADE BIAS TAPE OR BIAS TAPE MAKERS

Many patchwork stores now sell cute pre-made tapes that add another dimension to your bags and are easier and more foolproof to use. Occasionally, I like to make a bias tape out of one of the contrasting fabrics in my design – in this case you will need bias tape makers in a variety of widths.

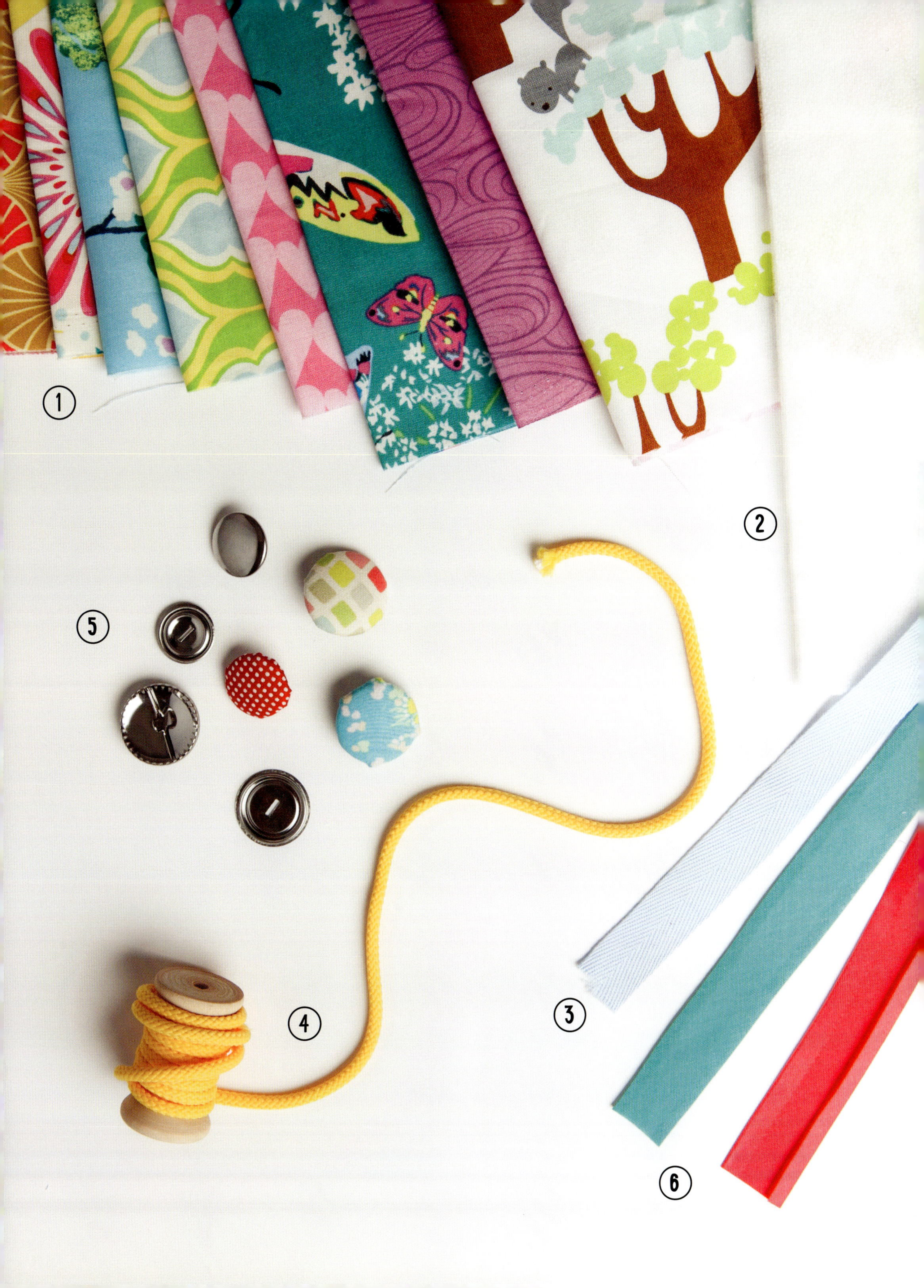
1
2
5
4
3
6

TOOLS & MATERIALS

HARDWARE

1. RINGS AND SLIDE ADJUSTERS

A number of my bags will call for handle rings and slide adjusters. I often refer to oblong rings or adjusters, but this is not a necessity for the projects. The width of the hardware is the main requirement and the oblong rings can often be replaced with square rings, D-rings or O-rings. Experiment with different rings to add a personal touch to your bags.

2. STRAP ADJUSTER

This is used on the Blue Skies Backpack only. It is slightly different from a slide adjuster, as it is designed to be used with a loose strap end. Due to angled bars on the adjuster, it will not adjust easily without intervention – important for use with a backpack.

3. MAGNETIC CLOSURES

Magnetic closures are great for making a bag or pockets more secure and user friendly. They are readily available and can be purchased in smaller and larger sizes; I like to use a thin closure so that I am not adding extra bulk to the bag. (See Inserting Magnetic Closures for instructions on the installation of these closures.)

4. ZIPS AND ZIPPER FEET

Zips can be used for bag tops or pockets and make a much more secure bag. I have used dress zips, chunky zips and open-end zips in my projects. Make sure you buy an open-end zip when stipulated, but feel free to substitute the thickness or variety. If you are a beginner or nervous of sewing zips, I recommend sticking to dress zips, but if you are more confident a chunky or metal-toothed zip may add a nice design element.

5. ZIPPER PULLS

These are a bit of fun if you want to add another, more professional, finish to your bags. There is a variety of zipper pulls available; I particularly like the cute Japanese leather pulls, as used in Ruffle Duffle.

6. SWIVEL HOOKS

These are hooks (that can swivel) attached to a handle ring, enabling you to have detachable handles. If you do not want a detachable handle, simply attach the handle to a standard handle ring in the normal fashion.

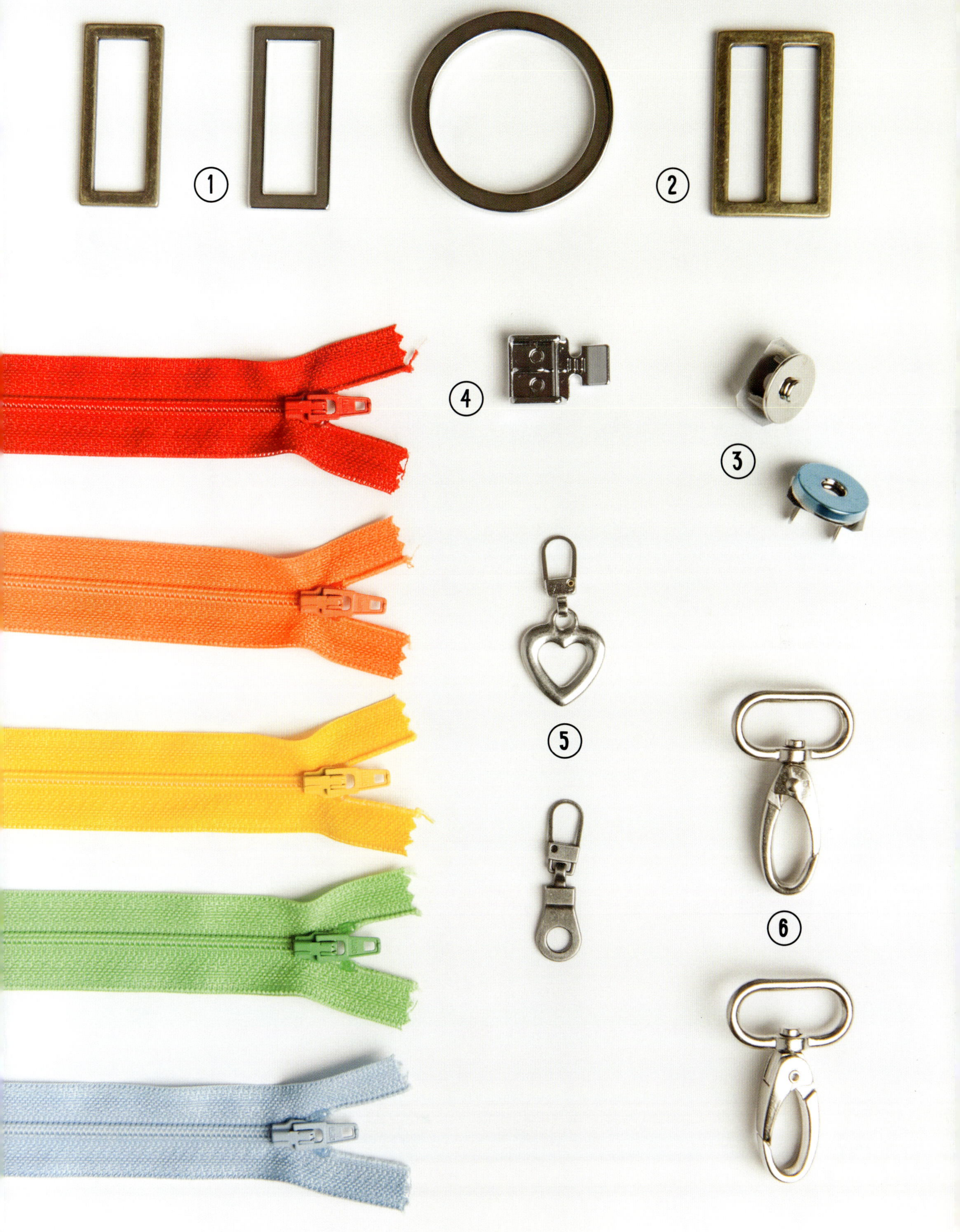
1
2
4
3
5
6

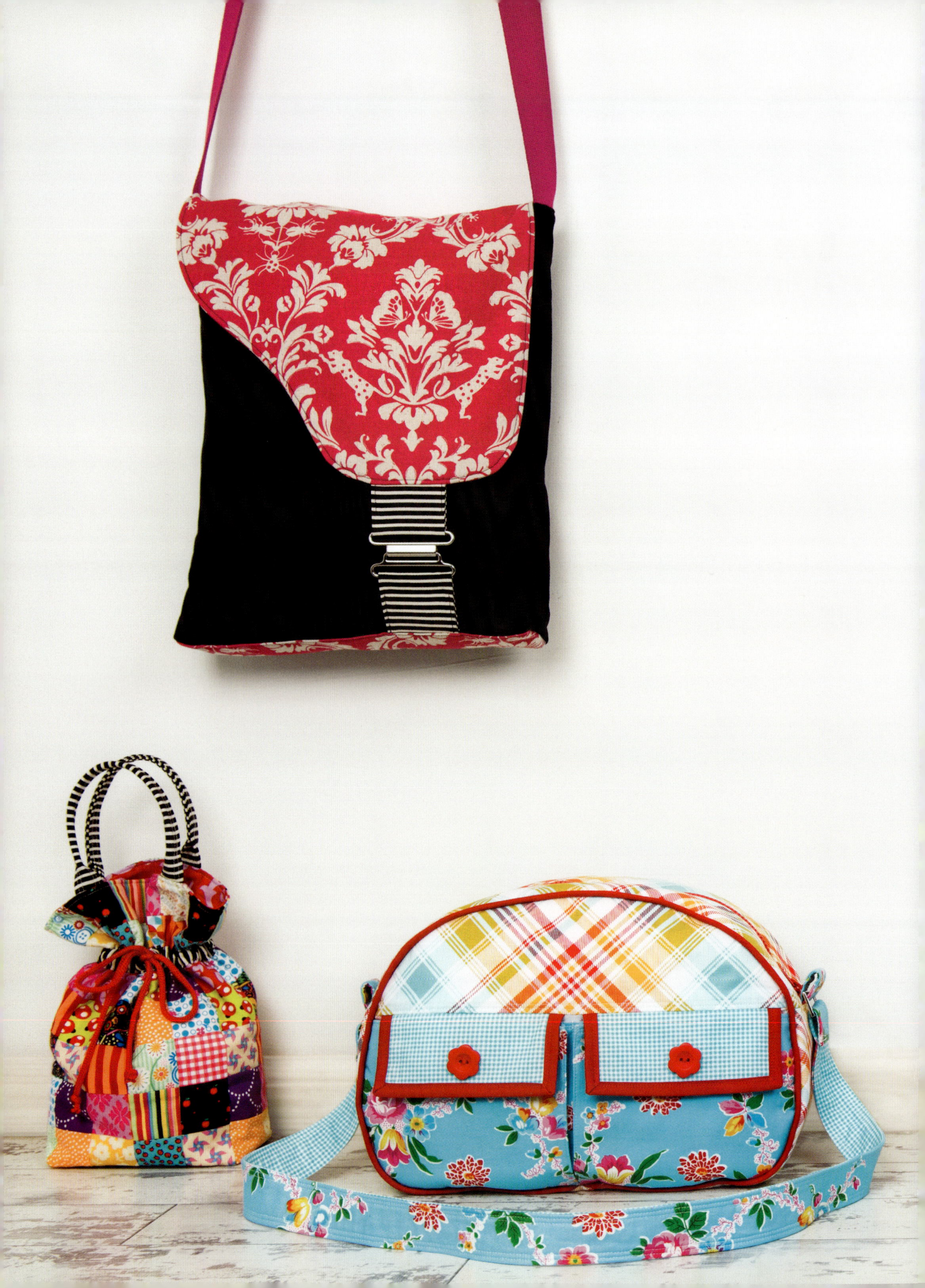

SEW CUTE BAGS

BEAUTIFUL BLOOMS HANDBAG

This fabulously floral handbag will sit perfectly on your arm. While it is compact, it still has plenty of room for your wallet, phone and all the other daily necessities. A handy outer pocket is perfect for those essential quick-reach items. It's so practical and pretty, you won't be able to resist!

SKILL RATING:

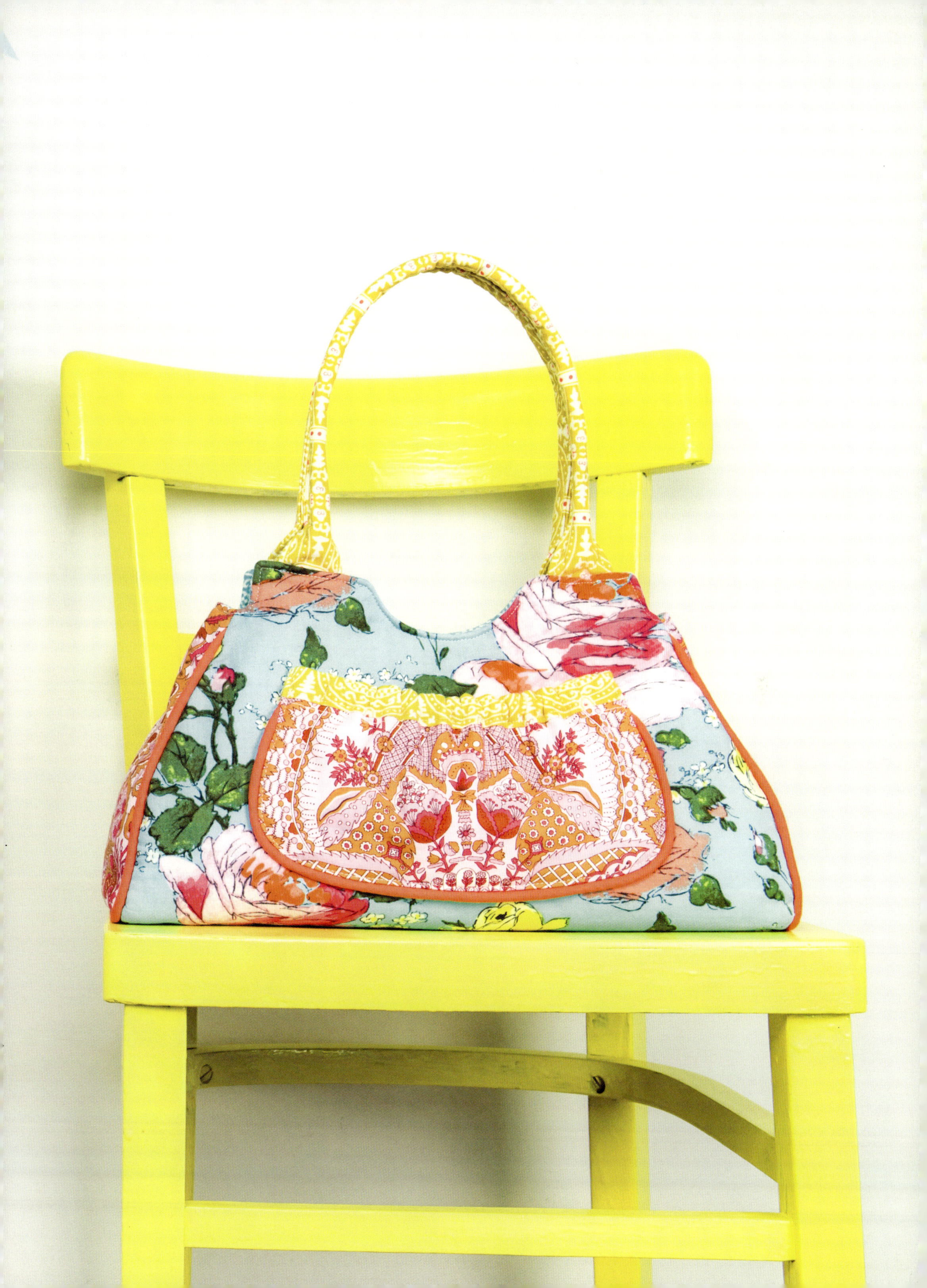

You will need

- 28cm (11in) blue fabric for main bag
- 28cm (11in) blue lining fabric
- 20cm (8in) pink fabric for pocket and side panels
- 15cm (6in) mustard fabric for handles and pocket top
- 1 fat quarter (18 x 22in) coral fabric to make piping (or 2m (2¼yd) bias tape)
- 75cm (30in) lightweight fusible fleece
- 2m (2¼yd) white cord to make piping
- 25cm (10in) of 1cm (⅜in) white elastic
- Magnetic closure

Finished size: 37 x 35.5cm (14½ x 14in) including handles

BEAUTIFUL BLOOMS HANDBAG

Cutting

1. Trace all of the Beautiful Blooms Handbag templates (see Pattern Pullout Sheet) onto tracing paper or template plastic, transferring all the markings and cutting them out around the traced lines.

2. From the main blue fabric, trace the main bag template twice and cut out along the traced lines.

3. From the blue lining fabric, trace the main bag template twice and cut out along the traced lines. Now trace the side panel template twice onto the remaining lining fabric and cut out along the traced lines.

4. From the pink fabric, trace the side panel template twice and cut out along the traced lines. Trace the pocket template twice onto the remaining fabric and cut out along the traced lines.

5. From the mustard fabric, cut two strips measuring 4.5 x 24cm (1¾ x 9½in) for the pocket top. Cut four strips measuring 5 x 42cm (2 x 16½in) for the handles.

6. From the coral fabric, cut three 3cm (1¼in) strips on the bias, each measuring 56cm (22in) in length.

7. From the lightweight fusible fleece, trace the main bag template twice onto the folded fleece and cut out along the traced lines to make four pieces. Next trace the side panel template twice onto the folded fleece and cut out along the traced lines to make four pieces. Cut four strips measuring 5 x 42cm (2 x 16½in) for the handles and set the rest aside.

Preparation

1. Take the main bag, lining, handle strip and your two pink side panel pieces and interface them all with your matching lightweight fusible fleece pieces. Take the two remaining side panel fleece pieces and shorten the top edges only by 1cm (⅜in). Use these to interface your lining side panel pieces.

2. Create three lengths of piping with the coral fabric bias strips and white cord (see Creating Piping).

TRY THIS!
Like more pockets? Why not whip up one or two more to sew onto your bag lining to create convenient internal pockets?

Construction

5mm (¼in) seam allowance included.

1. Take one of the pink pocket pieces and one of the mustard pocket top strips. Place these right sides together along the pocket top edge and sew in place. Press the seam to the pocket side then interface with the remaining fusible fleece. Topstitch along the pink pocket side of the seam only (see Useful Stitches). Sew the pocket lining and top strip together in the same way, but do not interface.

2. Take one of the lengths of piping and tack (baste) it along the raw pink edge of the interfaced pocket front piece only (see Useful Stitches). The raw edge of the piping should lie against the raw edge of the pocket fabric and the piping should taper away from the pocket just below the seam. Trim the ends neatly.

3. Place the pocket and pocket lining pieces right sides together and sew these together along all three edges of the mustard top strip only. Snip the corners and turn right side out. Topstitch the centre 16.5cm (6½in) of the top strip seam to create an elastic casing.

4. Now thread the white elastic through the elastic casing you just created in the pocket top. You can access this in-between the pocket and pocket lining layers. Sew a line of topstitching to secure the elastic at one end of the casing.

5. Pull the elastic through the remaining open end of the casing to create a nice gathering. The pocket top should now measure approximately 18cm (7in) in width. Secure the elastic at this end of the casing to create the elasticized pocket top. Trim any excess elastic from both sides of the casing.

6. Turn the pocket inside out again and tack (baste) the pocket and lining together all the way around the remaining raw edges with the piping between. Sew in place with the zipper foot as close to the piping as possible, leaving a 7.5cm (3in) gap along the bottom pocket edge for turning. Turn the pocket right side out and press, making sure that the turning gap is neatly folded in place. Position the pocket onto the bag front piece so that it is centred within the width and approximately 5cm (2in) down from the bag top edge. Now topstitch in place along the side and bottom edges.

7. Place the main bag front and back pieces on top of each other with right sides together. Sew together along the bottom edge of the bag and press the seam open. Repeat with the two lining pieces, this time leaving a 15cm (6in) gap in the centre for turning.

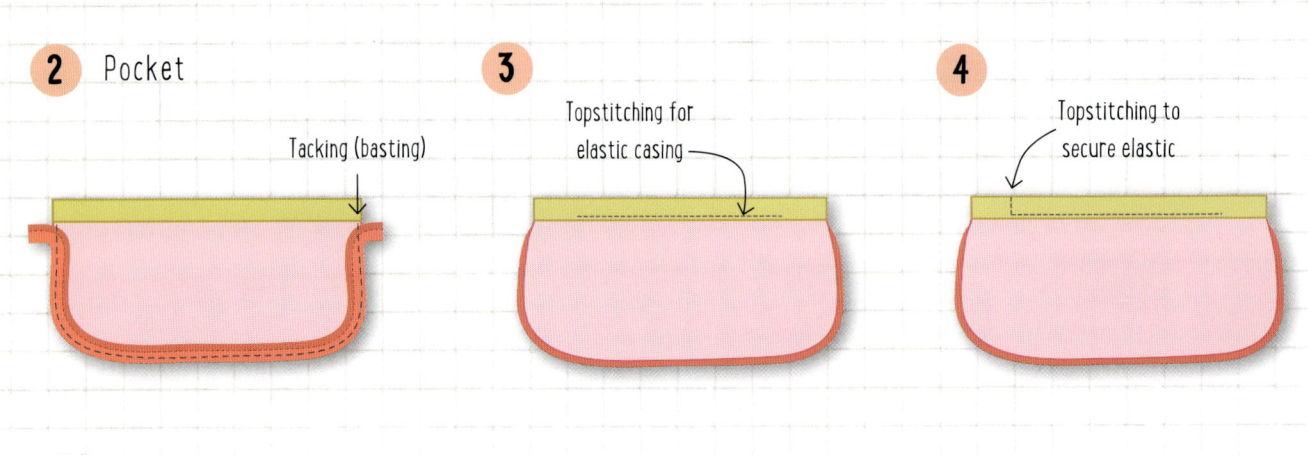

> *To insert elastic with ease, simply attach a safety pin to one end and use it to manoeuvre and guide the elastic through the casing.*

2 Pocket — Tacking (basting)

3 Topstitching for elastic casing

4 Topstitching to secure elastic

BEAUTIFUL BLOOMS HANDBAG

8. Place one of the lengths of piping right sides together along the side and bottom edges of one of the pink side panel pieces. The raw edge of the piping should lie against the raw edge of the fabric and the piping should taper away from the panel, 1.5cm (½in) from the top edge. Machine tack (baste) the piping into place as shown below, and trim the ends. Repeat with the other side panel piece.

9. Take one of the pink side panels (with piping) and the main bag piece. Tack the side panel into position by hand, right sides together, onto one of the side edges of the main bag piece. It is easier if you work from the centre out. When you are happy with the fit, sew the side panel into position. Repeat for the other side of the bag, then repeat with your bag lining and lining side panels.

10. Take two of the handle strips and place them on top of each other, right sides together. Sew together along three sides, leaving one short end open for turning. Turn right side out (see Turning Handles), trim off the sewn end and press well. Topstitch the handle along both long edges. Fold the handle onto itself all the way along the length and then topstitch it in this folded position, starting and ending 4cm (1½in) from both raw ends. Topstitch this together by stitching over your previous topstitching. Repeat to create the second handle piece.

11. Place one of the handles right sides together on top of the bag front. Machine tack the handle ends in position, close to the raw edges. Repeat with the second handle at the bag back.

12. Keeping the main bag right side out and the bag lining wrong side out, place the main bag inside the lining bag. Carefully sew all the way around the top of the bag, ensuring that you capture the bag handle ends within the stitching. Snip angles, curved edges and corners for flexibility. Ensure you snip a few times in the angles where the side panels meet the main bag.

It is important to snip your seams at times to allow the bag to turn right side out evenly and neatly without any puckering. Ensure that you do not snip too close to the sewn line as this may weaken or break your seams.

13. Turn the bag right side out through the gap in the base of the lining and push the lining inside the main bag. Press, and then topstitch the opening all the way around the top edges of the bag.

14. Insert the magnetic closure into the centre of the lining, approximately 1.5cm (½in) down from the top edge (see Inserting Magnetic Closures). Ladder stitch the opening in the lining closed (see Useful Stitches).

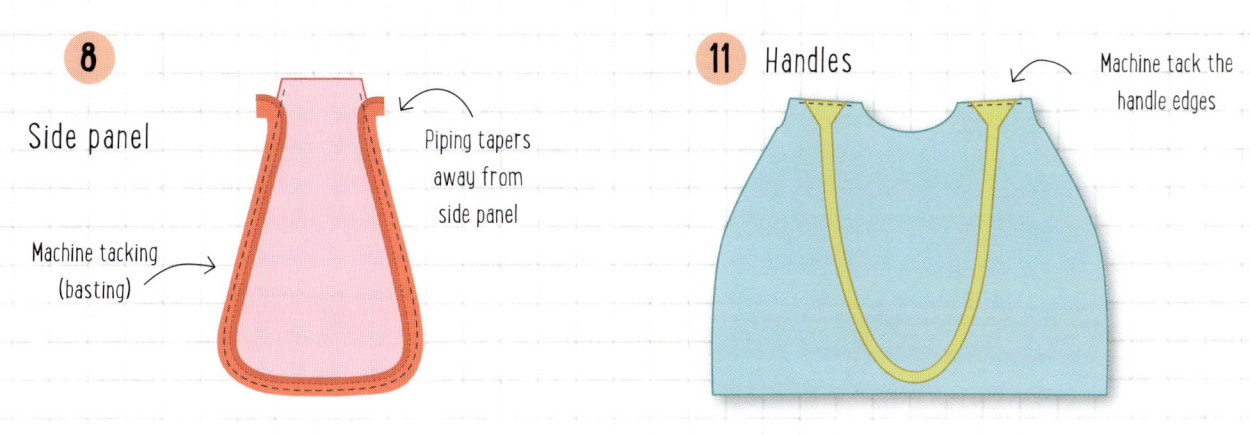

8 Side panel — Machine tacking (basting) — Piping tapers away from side panel

11 Handles — Machine tack the handle edges

CITY NIGHTS CLUTCH

Every girl needs a whole drawer full of chic clutches! I love picking out the perfect clutch to complement my outfit for a fun night out with friends. This eye-catching floral print with its cute crochet flower button makes a bold statement. Mix and match your favourite fabrics to that new outfit to add a splash of colour and fun.

SKILL RATING: 👜 👜 👜

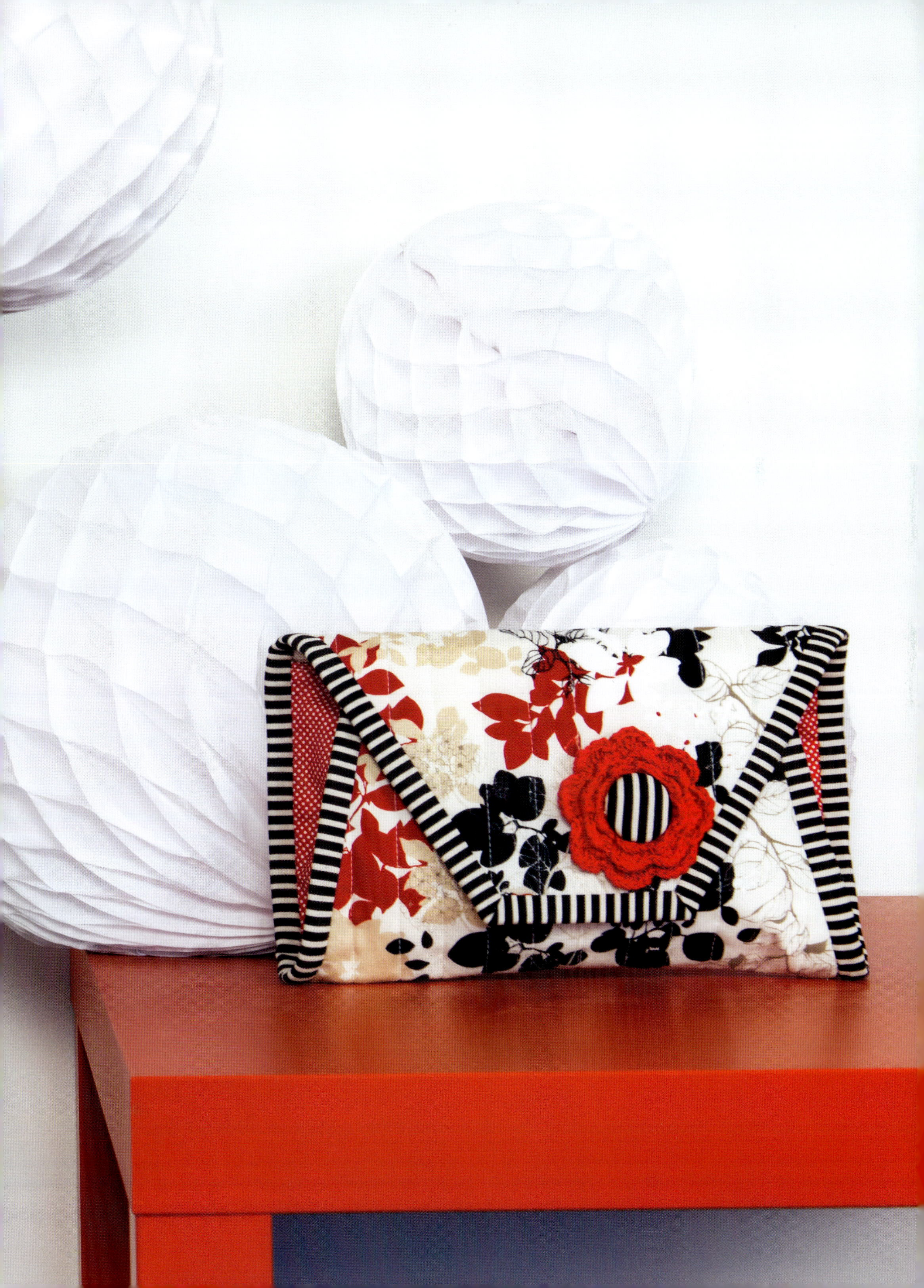

You will need

- 28cm (11in) black and red home décor weight print fabric for main bag (if you are using a directional print you will require extra fabric)
- 18 x 50cm (7 x 20in) red micro spot fabric for side gussets
- 12.5cm (5in) black stripe fabric for binding and button
- 28cm (11in) lightweight fusible fleece
- 28 x 50cm (11 x 20in) medium/heavy iron-on interfacing
- Chalk pencil or erasable marker
- Large crocheted flower
- Self-covering button, approximately 2.5cm (1in) in diameter
- Magnetic closure

Finished size: 16.5 x 27cm (6½ x 10½in)

CITY NIGHTS CLUTCH

Cutting

1. Trace all of the City Nights Clutch templates (see Pattern Pullout Sheet) onto tracing paper or template plastic, transferring all the markings and cutting them out around the traced lines.

2. From the black and red main home décor weight print fabric, trace the main clutch template twice. Cut out along the traced lines.

3. From the red micro spot fabric, trace the side gusset template four times and cut out along the traced lines.

4. From the black stripe fabric, cut one strip measuring 5cm (2in) x the full width and another strip measuring 5 x 20cm (2 x 8in).

5. From the lightweight fusible fleece, trace the main clutch template once and cut out along the traced lines. Next trace the side gusset template twice and cut out.

6. From the iron-on interfacing, trace the main clutch template once and cut out along the traced lines.

Preparation

1. Interface one main clutch piece and two side gusset pieces with lightweight fusible fleece. Interface the remaining main clutch piece with the iron-on interfacing.

2. Interface a scrap of black stripe fabric with lightweight fusible fleece and use this to cover your self-covering button, following the manufacturer's instructions.

TRY THIS!
Feel adventurous and want to make a patchwork clutch? Simply piece a panel of fabric with your favourite patchwork piecing and use this to cut your clutch template from.

Construction

5mm (¼in) seam allowance included.

1. Take the main clutch piece with fusible fleece and insert the female side of the magnetic closure into the right side of the panel in the position marked on the Pattern Pullout Sheet (see Inserting Magnetic Closures). Repeat to position the male side of the magnetic closure on the clutch lining piece with interfacing.

2. Place the two main clutch pieces on top of each other, right sides out. Pin then machine tack (baste) the two pieces together close to the raw edges (see Useful Stitches).

3. Using a chalk pencil or erasable marker, rule a line down the centre of the clutch panel from top to bottom. Now rule lines parallel to this at 2cm (¾in) intervals, as shown below. Following the ruled lines, quilt the clutch panel, making sure that you start and stop before the magnetic closure pieces on the central line of stitching.

To ensure neat and even quilting, start from the centre quilting line out and sew each line of quilting in the same direction.

4. Take one of the 5 x 20cm (2 x 8in) black stripe binding strips. Either use a 2.5cm (1in) bias tape maker or make your own binding by folding the binding strip in half along the length, right side out, and pressing. Now fold the long raw edges into the fold and press again. Use this binding strip to bind the front edge of the clutch panel (see Topstitch Binding).

5. Take one of the side gusset pieces with fusible fleece and sew the dart into place at the bottom (see Sewing Darts). Repeat using a side gusset piece without fleece. Place the two gusset pieces on top of each other, right sides together and sew together along the top straight edge only.

6. Turn the gusset pieces right sides out so that they both sit evenly on top of each other. Press and then topstitch along the top sewn edge. Tack (baste) the remaining raw edges together.

7. Starting at one corner of the clutch front and ensuring the dart in the gusset meets the marked star on the template sheet, ease the gusset into place, lining sides together, along the side edge of

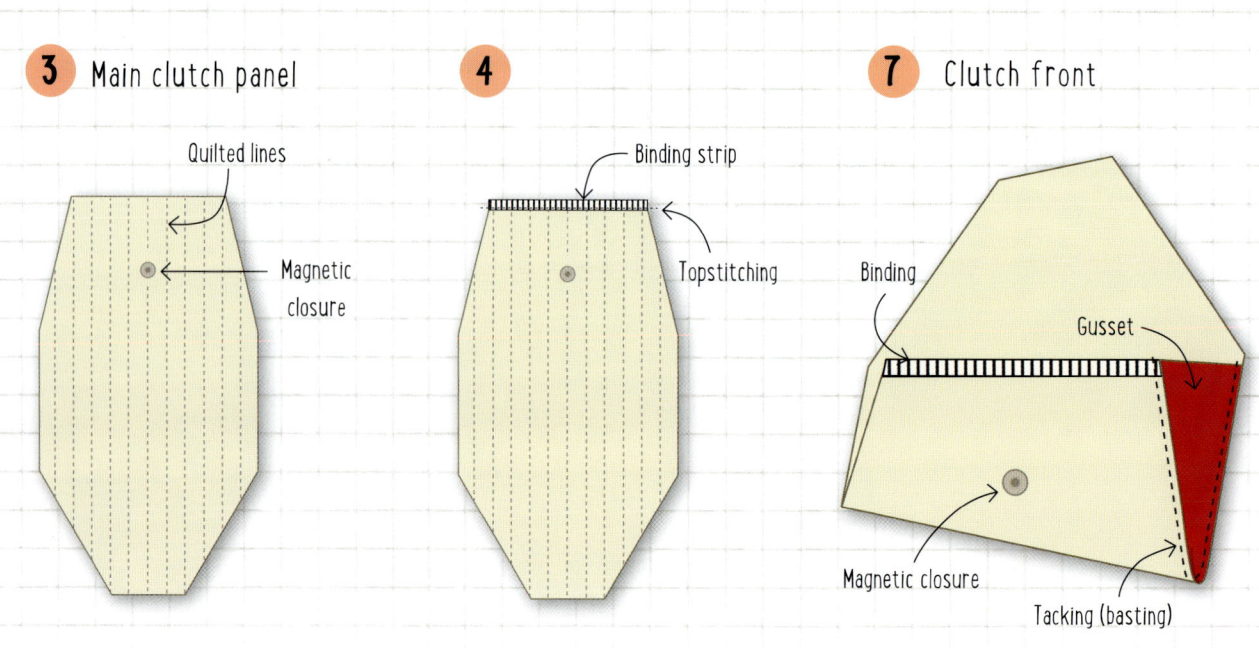

3 Main clutch panel
- Quilted lines
- Magnetic closure

4
- Binding strip
- Topstitching

7 Clutch front
- Binding
- Gusset
- Magnetic closure
- Tacking (basting)

28

CITY NIGHTS CLUTCH

the clutch so that all raw edges meet. Machine tack (baste) in place. This will create the bag section of the clutch. Repeat Steps 5–7 to create the other side gusset.

When you reach the bottom of the gussets go slowly, taking care to flatten out the bottom layer of fabric as you go to avoid puckering.

8. Take the strip of black stripe binding fabric. Use a 2.5cm (1in) bias tape maker to create your strip of binding or follow Step 4 instructions to create your binding manually. Unfold one end of the binding strip, fold the raw end in by 5mm (¼in) and press. Then refold the binding in place and press well to create a neat end.

9. Open out one long folded edge of the binding. Line the raw edge of the folded in end up with the top corner of the clutch front, right sides together. Sew the binding into place along the crease in the binding, 1.5cm (½in) from the raw edges. Sew in place, all the way around the raw clutch edge until you reach the other side of the clutch front. When you reach the corners of the opening flap, mitre the corners (see Standard Continuous Binding). At the end, trim the binding 5mm (¼in) longer than needed, fold the end in and sew the neat folded end in place.

10. Fold the binding evenly over to the other side of the clutch, enclosing the raw clutch edges, much like you would to bind a quilt. Neatly ladder stitch (see Useful Stitches) the folded binding edge in place by hand all the way around the clutch.

11. Ladder stitch the folded front and back sections of the binding together at the front corners, as shown in the photograph (below).

12. Place the covered button over the centre of the large crocheted flower. Sew the button into place, also taking the stitches through the crocheted flower to secure all the layers together.

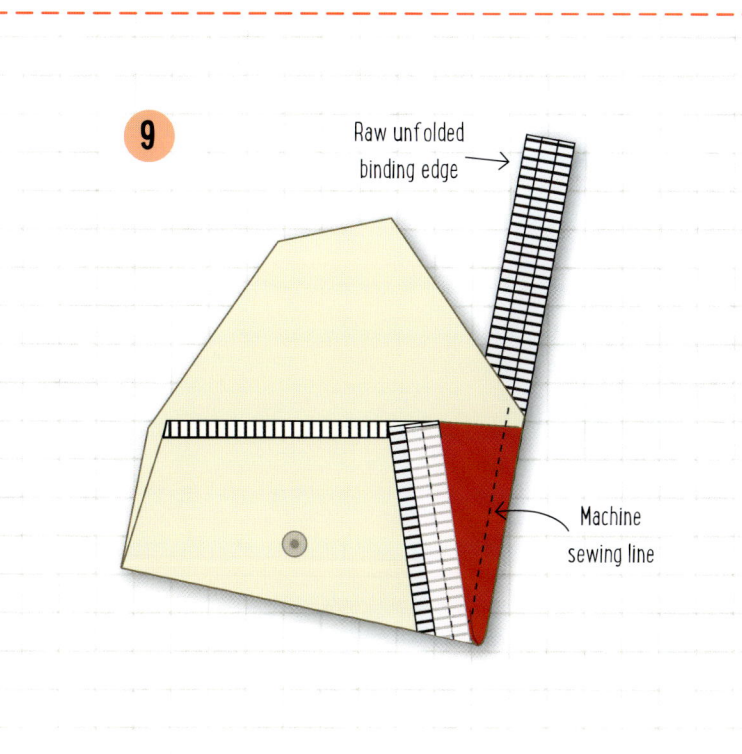

9
Raw unfolded binding edge →

Machine sewing line

CUTE CARRY-ALL

Introducing the true bag-a-holic's bag with room for absolutely everything! This versatile carry-all could be used as an oversized handbag, a project bag or a super stylish changing bag. With a large zipped front pocket and a generous double pocket inside, you can secure any precious items while the main bag remains easily accessible.

SKILL RATING: 👜👜

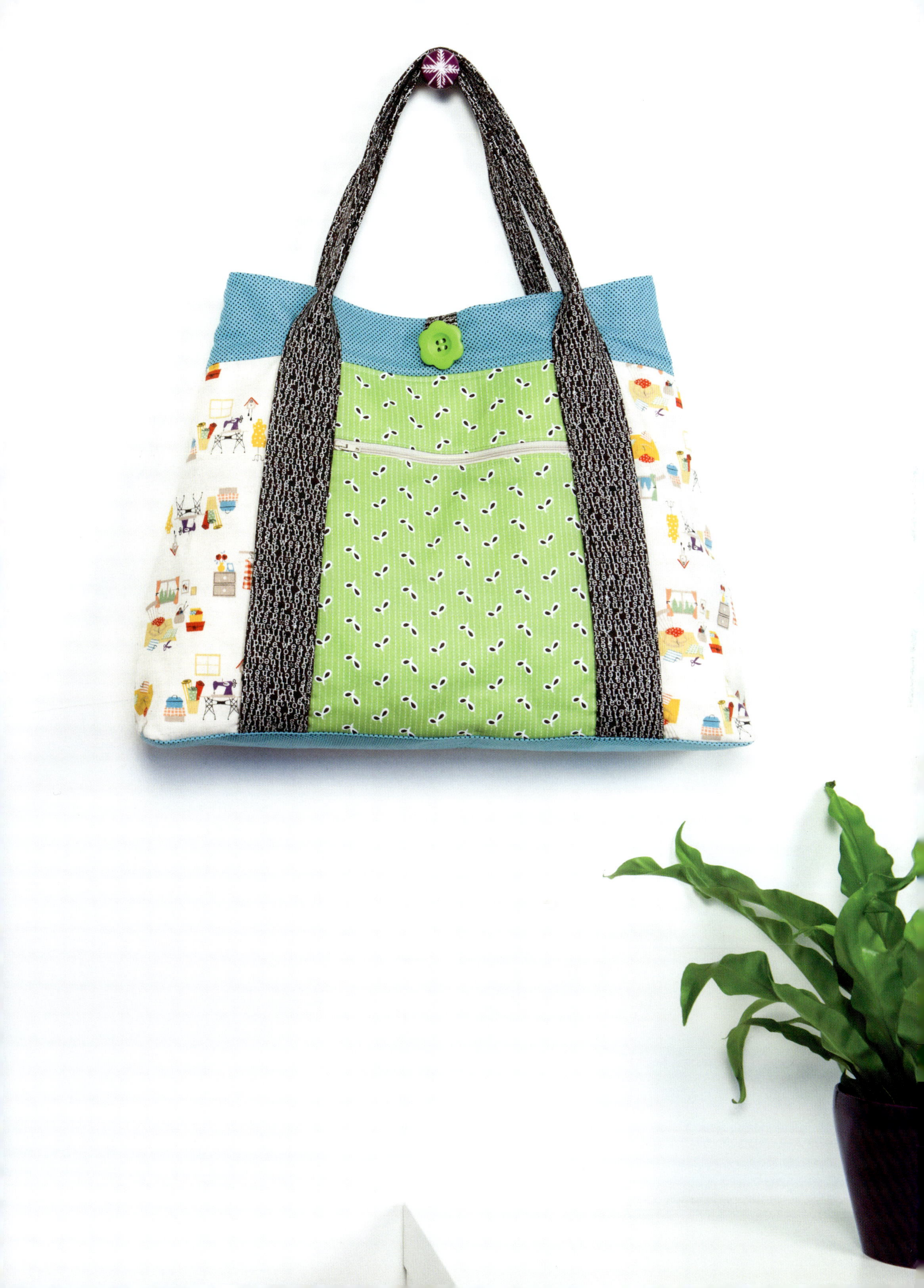

You will need

- 75cm (30in) cream home décor weight fabric for bag front, back and lining
- 25cm (10in) green print fabric for front zipped pocket
- 33cm (13in) blue spot fabric for bag top and base
- 89cm (35in) brown text fabric for handles, internal pocket and closure
- 2m (2¼yd) lightweight fusible fleece
- 9 x 56cm (3½ x 22in) heavy iron-on interfacing
- Zip, at least 28cm (11in) in length
- Large green button

Finished size: 50 x 48cm (20 x 18¾in) including handles

CUTE CARRY-ALL

Cutting

1. Trace all of the Cute Carry-All templates (see Pattern Pullout Sheet) onto tracing paper or template plastic, transferring all the markings and cutting them out around the traced lines.

2. From the cream home décor weight fabric, trace the main bag template four times and cut out along the traced lines.

3. From the green print fabric, cut two pieces measuring 25 x 27.5cm (10 x 11in) and another two pieces measuring 25 x 8cm (10 x 3¼in).

4. From the blue spot fabric, cut one strip measuring 11.5 x 55cm (4½ x 22in). Trace the bag top template four times onto the remaining fabric and cut out along the traced lines.

5. From the brown text print fabric, trace the main bag template twice and cut out along the traced lines to make the internal pocket. For the handles, cut eight strips measuring 6.5 x 64cm (2½ x 25¼in). Cut another strip measuring 4.5 x 14cm (1¾ x 5½in) for the button closure.

6. From the lightweight fusible fleece, cut a piece measuring 25 x 27.5cm (10 x 11in) and another measuring 25 x 8cm (10 x 3¼in). Now cut one strip measuring 9 x 55cm (3½ x 22in) and eight more strips measuring 6.5 x 60cm (2½ x 23½in) for the handles. Trace the main bag template once and cut out along the traced lines for the internal pocket. Set aside any remaining fabric.

Preparation

1. Take one each of the green print panels, one of the brown pocket pieces and all of the handle strips and interface these with your matching lightweight fusible fleece pieces. You will notice that the handle fleece is shorter than the fabric strips – this is intentional. Interface so that the fleece starts at one end edge but does not cover the full length at the other end.

TRY THIS!
I enjoyed playing with a fun combination of fabrics on this project. Feel free to play and have fun or alternatively be as co-ordinated as you like!

Construction

5mm (¼in) seam allowance included.

1. Place the two 25 x 27.5cm (10 x 11in) pieces of green print fabric on top of each other, right sides together. Create a sandwich by placing the centred zip in-between these two pocket layers along one 25cm (10in) edge. The interfaced fabric panel should be positioned right sides together with the zip. Pin in place then sew together with the zipper foot, as shown below. Open the fabric away from the zip, press and topstitch (see Useful Stitches).

2. Place the two 25 x 8cm (10 x 3¼in) pieces of green print fabric on top of each other, right sides together. Place the remaining side of the zip between these two pocket layers along one 25cm (10in) edge. Making sure that the interfaced piece is right sides together with the zip and this sandwich is equally in line with the layers sewn in Step 1 below, pin and then sew together with your zipper foot. Open the fabric away from the zip, press and topstitch.

3. Making sure that the zip pull is within the pocket section, secure the ends of the zip close to the edge of the fabric with some backward and forward stitches, as shown below. Trim the excess zip at the pocket edge.

4. Place one of the cream main bag pieces right side up on your work surface. Position the pocket panel centrally on top of this and machine tack (baste) around all four edges (see Useful Stitches).

5. Take one of the blue bag top pieces and place it on top of the bag front, right sides together. The bottom straight edge of the bag top should meet the top edge of the main bag piece with pocket. Sew in place and press. Interface the complete bag front with the remaining fusible fleece and topstitch the bag top seam. Repeat with the remaining three main bag and bag top pieces.

If the pocket panel is a little higher than the main bag piece, simply trim away any excess.

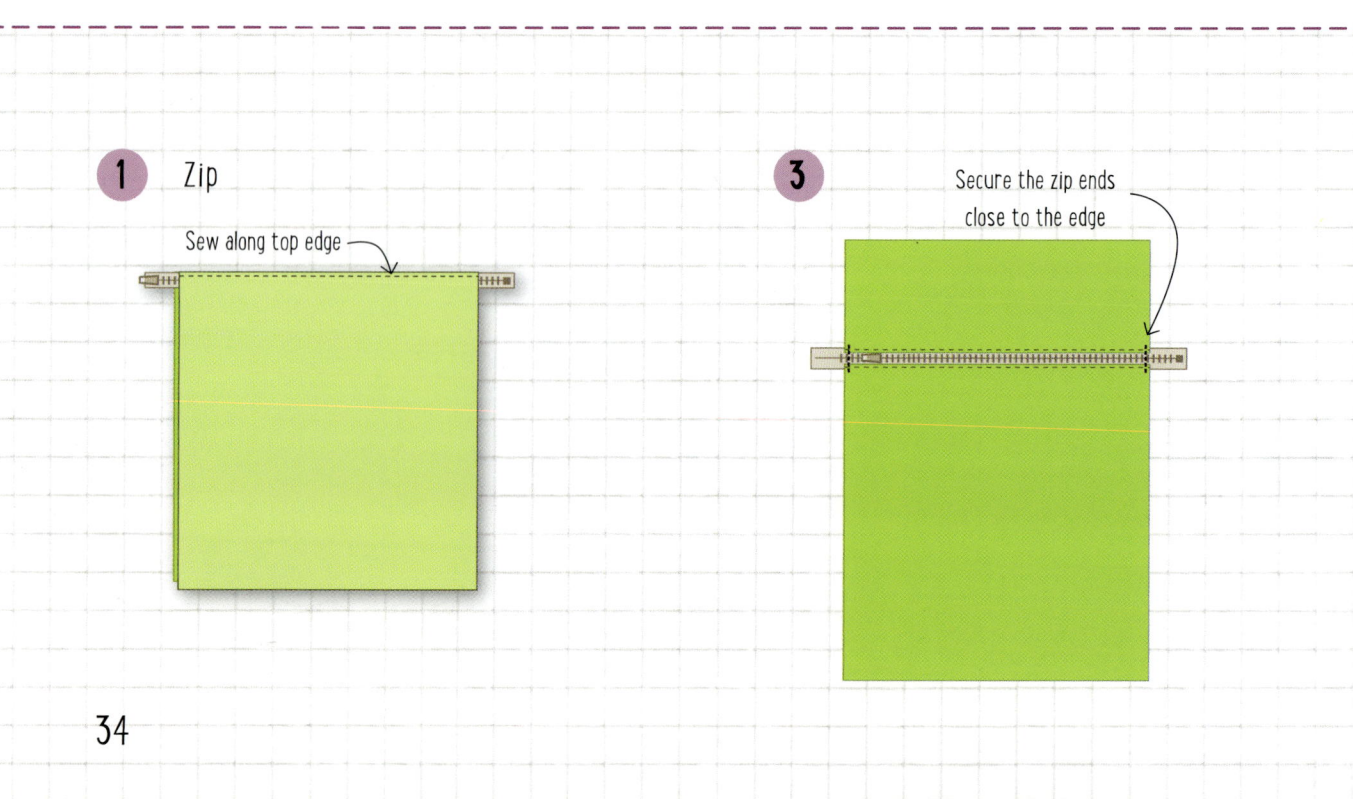

1 Zip
Sew along top edge

3 Secure the zip ends close to the edge

CUTE CARRY-ALL

6. Take two of the brown handle strips and sew them together along the short ends with fleece. Repeat with the remaining six handle strips so that you now have four interfaced strips measuring 127 x 6.5cm (50 x 2½in).

7. Place two of the handle strips on top of each other, right sides together. Sew together along three edges, leaving one of the short ends open. Turn right side out (see Turning Handles), trim the sewn end and press well.

8. Place the bag front on your work surface, right side up. Pin the handle into position as shown below, so that it covers the side seams of the pocket panel. Both raw ends of the handle should meet the bottom raw edge of the bag front. Topstitch the handle into place, stopping approximately 1.5cm (½in) up from the bag top seam.

9. Fold the remaining unattached handle section onto itself along the entire length. Topstitch the handle in this folded position, starting and ending 4cm (1½in) from where the handle is attached to the bag front. Topstitch a line of stitches parallel to the first line of topstitching every 3mm (⅛in), as shown in the photograph below, to give strength to the strap. Repeat Steps 7–9 with the bag back.

10. Place the bag front and back pieces on top of each other, right sides together. Sew together along the bottom edge only.

11. To make the bag base panel, iron the 9 x 55cm (3½ x 22in) piece of fusible fleece to the centre of the 11.5 x 55cm (4½ x 22in) blue spot fabric panel so you have 1.5cm (½in) of fabric on either side of the fleece. Fuse the heavy interfacing evenly over the fleece for extra thickness and strength. Fold the extra 1.5cm (½in) of fabric on both sides over the edges of the interfacing and press in place.

TRY THIS!

Topstitching multiple lines of stitching at close intervals along a handle creates a fabulously strong handle. Why not try this on other bag patterns to add extra strength?

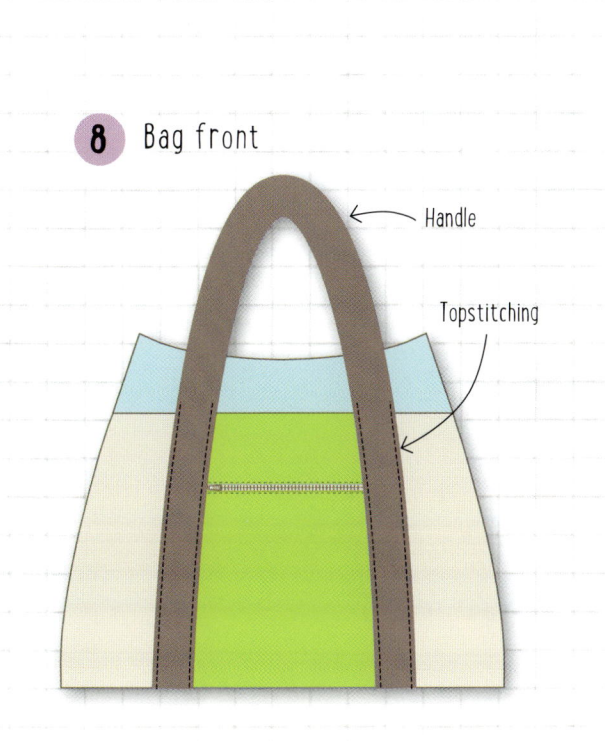

8 Bag front

→ Handle

→ Topstitching

12. Open the main bag out and lay it flat, right side up, so that the bottom seam is lying flat on your work surface. Centre the base panel, right side up, over the seam as shown below, so that 4.5cm (1¾in) of the base will go over the bag front and 4.5cm (1¾in) over the bag back. Make sure the folded under 1.5cm (½in) on both sides of the base panel remains underneath. Pin in place and topstitch onto the bag along both edges.

13. Position the bag front and back right sides together so both the top edges and side edges meet evenly. Sew the sides together, starting at the top edge and ending when you reach the base panel.

14. Keeping the bag inside out, follow the box corner technique (see Box Corners), sewing across where the triangle measures 9cm (3½in) – from one edge of the base panel to the other. Repeat for the other corner. Trim the excess fabric approximately 1.5cm (½in) outside the sewn line.

The fabric in the corners will be very thick, so take care with your needle and sew over the stitching a few times for added strength.

15. Place the two brown pocket pieces right sides together and sew together along the top straight edge. Open right sides out, press and topstitch along the top sewn edge with two rows of stitching.

16. Take one of the bag lining pieces and place it right side up on your work surface. Position the internal pocket on top of this so that the side and bottom raw edges all meet. Sew the pocket neatly into place along the side and bottom edges. Sew a line of topstitching from top to bottom down the centre of the bag to create a divided pocket if desired.

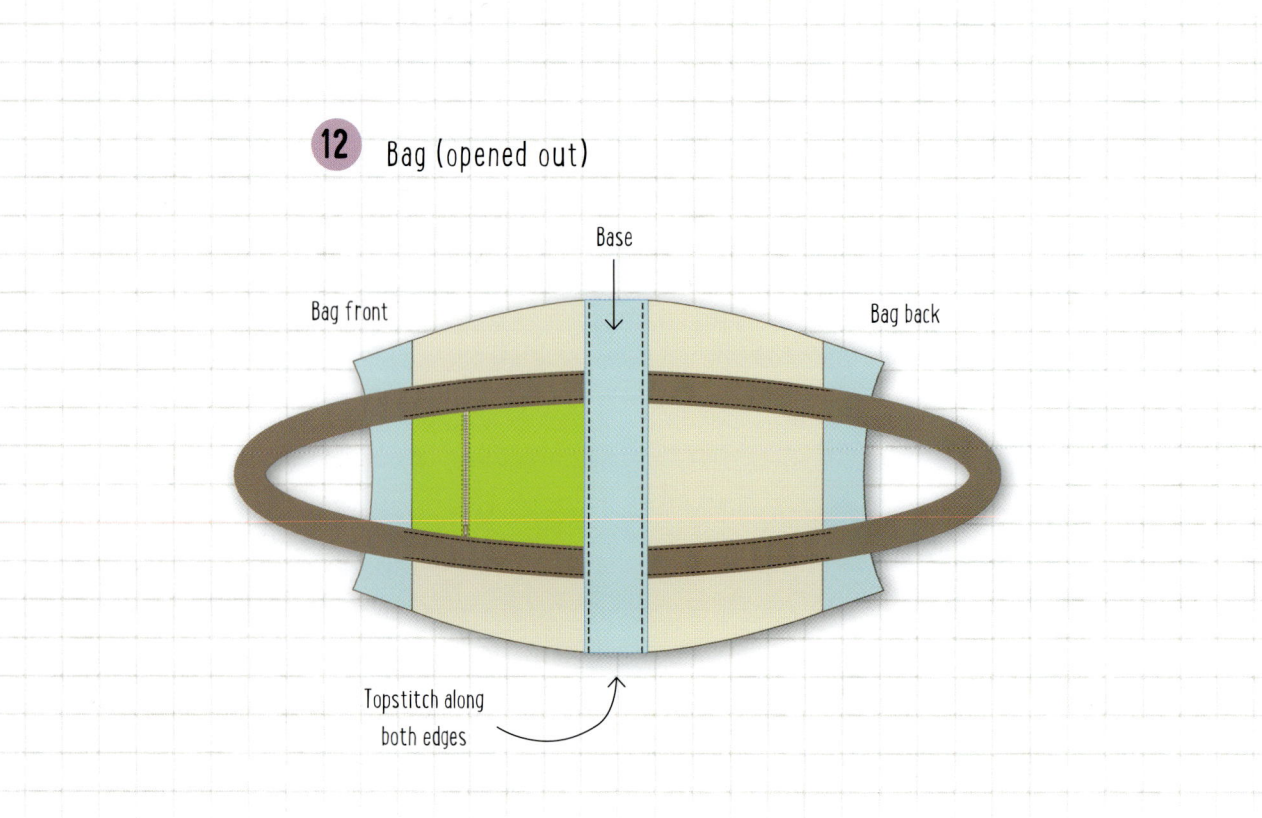

12 Bag (opened out)

Bag front | Base | Bag back

Topstitch along both edges

CUTE CARRY-ALL

17. Place both bag lining pieces on top of each other, right sides together. Sew together along the side and bottom edges, leaving a 20cm (8in) gap in the centre of the bottom edge for turning. Keeping the lining bag inside out, follow the box corner technique (see Box Corners), sewing across where the triangle measures 9cm (3½in). Repeat for the other corner.

18. Take the 4.5 x 14cm (1¾ x 5½in) fabric button closure strip and fold this in half along the length, right side out. Press, then turn the raw edges into the centre fold and press again. Topstitch the loose edges of the strip together to secure. Fold the strip in half, forming a triangle at the fold to create a loop and topstitch the triangle to secure, as seen below.

19. Place the button closure loop right sides together at the centre top of the lining back (with pocket) so that the raw edges meet. Machine tack (baste) in place.

20. Keeping the main bag right side out and the bag lining right side in, place the main bag inside the lining bag. Push the handles inside the two layers so that they are well clear of the top edge and pin all the way around the top edge. Carefully sew all the way around the top of the bag, catching the closure in this seam. Turn the bag right side out through the hole in the bottom of the lining and push the lining inside the main bag. Topstitch along the top bag edge.

21. Sew the button in the desired position at the centre top of the bag front, accessing this through the gap in the lining. Ladder stitch the turning gap closed (see Useful Stitches).

TRY THIS!
Have fun with your button selections – you will be surprised by how much added appeal they can give your favourite bag designs.

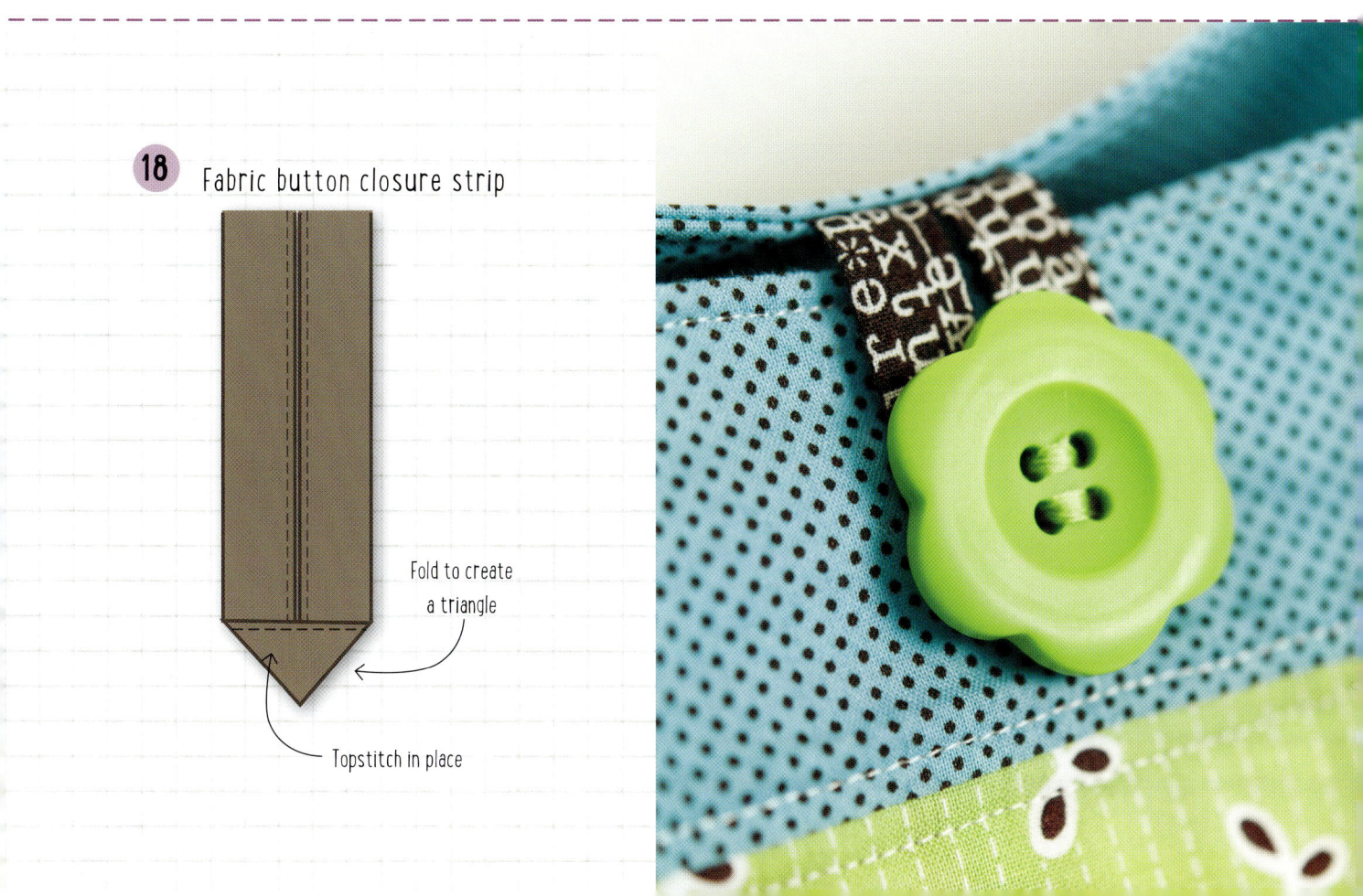

18 Fabric button closure strip

Fold to create a triangle

Topstitch in place

BLUE SKIES BACKPACK

This charming, casual backpack is sure to be your favourite accessory on your next shopping expedition or day trip. Completely secure, it cannot be opened when on your back, making it ideal to carry all those valuable essentials safely in busy crowds. The front pocket is handy for any items that you need quick access to on your travels.

SKILL RATING: 👜👜👜

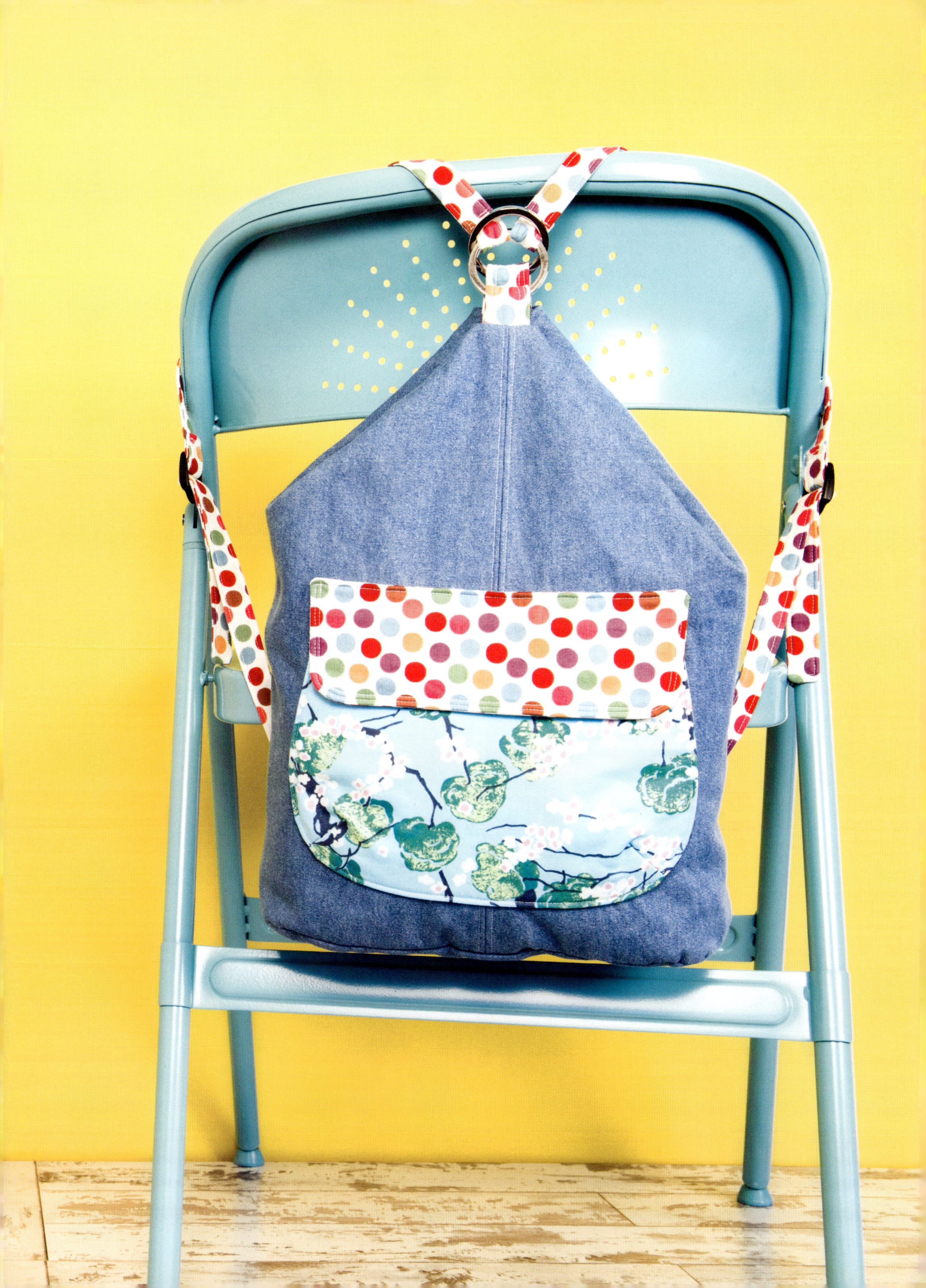

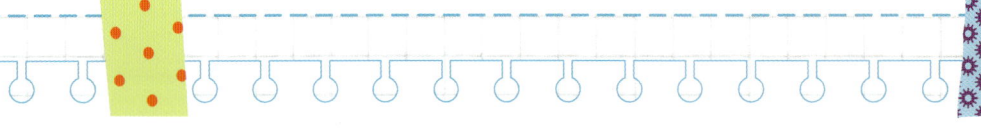

You will need

- 91.5cm (36in) lightweight denim or any other desired fabric for outer bag and lining
- 30 x 40cm (12 x 16in) blue floral fabric for pocket
- 25cm (10in) colourful spot print fabric for pocket flap
- 80cm (32in) lightweight fusible fleece
- Two large 5cm (2in) rings
- Matching dress zip, 40cm (16in) in length
- Two 2cm (¾in) black strap adjusters
- Two magnetic closures

Finished size: 43 x 30cm (17 x 12in) excluding handles

BLUE SKIES BACKPACK

Cutting

1. Trace all of the Blue Skies Backpack templates (see Pattern Pullout Sheet) onto tracing paper or template plastic, transferring all the markings and cutting them out around the traced lines.

2. From the main lightweight denim or substitute fabric, trace the main bag template four times and cut out along the traced lines. Now trace the bag base template twice and cut out along the traced lines.

3. From the blue floral fabric, trace the pocket template twice and cut out along the traced lines.

4. From the colourful spot print fabric, cut out four strips measuring 51 x 3.5cm (20 x 1⅜in), four strips measuring 47 x 3.5cm (18½ x 1⅜in) and another four strips measuring 7.5 x 4.5cm (3 x 1¾in). Next trace the pocket flap template twice and cut out along the traced lines.

5. From the lightweight fusible fleece, trace the main bag template twice, then bag base template once, the pocket template once and the pocket flap template once. Cut out along the traced lines for each template. Now cut out the following strips: two measuring 51 x 3.5cm (20 x 1⅜in), two measuring 47 x 3.5cm (18½ x 1⅜in) and finally two measuring 4.5 x 7.5cm (1¾ x 3in).

Preparation

1. Trim the top and top corner edges of the main bag interfacing pieces by 6mm (¼in). Interface two of the main bag pieces so that the bottom edges of the interfacing and bag pieces match and the top seam allowance is not interfaced.

2. Interface one of each of the main bag base, pocket and pocket flap pieces and half of the colourful spot strips with the matching lightweight fusible fleece pieces.

3. Insert the female halves of the magnetic closures into the interfaced pocket piece and the male halves into the interfaced pocket flap piece, following the template markings (see Inserting Magnetic Closures).

41

Construction

5mm (¼in) seam allowance included.

1. Take the two pocket pieces and sew all of the darts into place (see Sewing Darts). Place the two pocket pieces on top of each other, right sides together. Sew together along all the edges, leaving a 7.5cm (3in) gap along the bottom edge for turning. Snip the corners, turn and press. Topstitch the top edge with a double row of stitches (see Useful Stitches).

2. Place the two pocket flap pieces on top of each other, right sides together. Sew together along all the edges, leaving a 7.5cm (3in) gap along the top straight edge for turning. Snip the corners, turn and press, ensuring that you turn in the turning gap neatly. Topstitch the curved side and bottom flap edges with a double row of stitches.

3. Place the two main bag pieces (with interfacing) on top of each other, right sides together, and sew together along one side edge only. Open and press, then topstitch the sewn seam along both edges. Please note that this seam will now be positioned at the bag centre front.

There is no need to hand stitch the turning gaps on the pocket pieces closed; simply ensure that the gap edges are folded in and neatly pressed. When you topstitch this section onto the bag, the gaps will be automatically secured.

4. Take the main bag and lay it open, right side up, on your work surface. Place the pocket centrally over the seam, approximately 5cm (2in) up from the bottom edge, as shown. Topstitch in place along the side and bottom edges.

5. Take the pocket flap and attach the magnetic closures to the ones on the pocket. Pin the top edge of the closure flap in this position and topstitch in place, as shown.

6. Tack (baste) (see Useful Stitches) one edge of the zip, right sides together to the top raw edge of one side of the main bag as shown. Use a zipper foot to sew the zip in place. Open, press and topstitch the seam.

7. Open the zip then tack the remaining zip edge to the remaining top edge of the other side of the bag. Sew in place then press and topstitch.

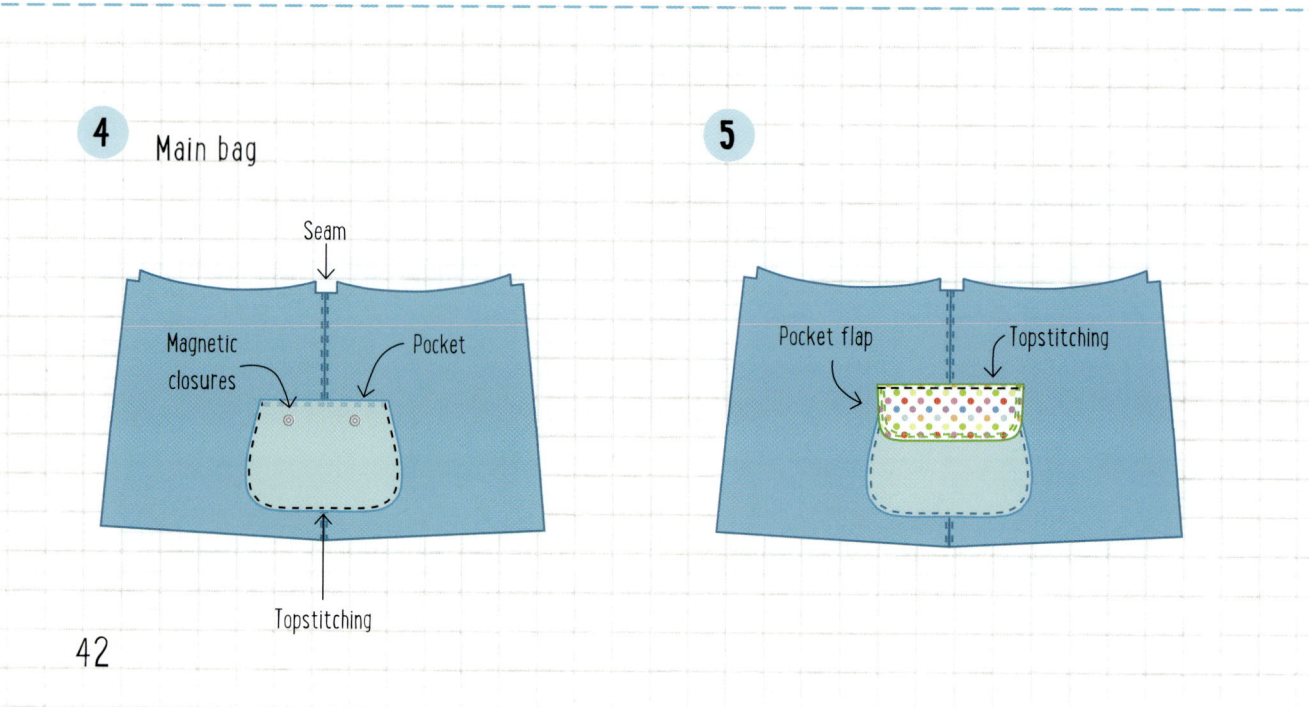

4 Main bag

Seam
Magnetic closures
Pocket
Topstitching

5

Pocket flap
Topstitching

BLUE SKIES BACKPACK

8. Fold the two sides of the bag so they are right sides together again and the remaining side edges now meet. Sew the remaining side edges together. Topstitch along both seam sides as you did for the bag front (this will take some care and patience!).

9. Place one interfaced and one non-interfaced 51 x 3.5cm (20 x 1⅜in) spot print strip on top of each other, right sides together. Sew together along all four edges, leaving a 7.5cm (3in) gap in one long edge for turning. Snip the corners and turn (see Turning Handles). Press well and topstitch along all edges. Repeat to create the second shoulder piece. Repeat for the 47 x 3.5cm (18½ x 1⅜in) spot fabric strips, this time leaving one short end open for turning to make two adjustable strap pieces.

10. Place one of the interfaced and one of the non-interfaced spot fabric strips measuring 7.5 x 4.5cm (3 x 1¾in) on top of each other, right sides together. Sew together along both long edges, leaving the ends open for turning. Turn, press well and topstitch along both sewn edges with a double row of stitches. Repeat to create the second ring holder piece. Thread a ring holder piece through one of the rings, folding it onto itself to capture the ring. Machine tack (baste) the raw edges together. Repeat with the remaining ring holder and ring.

11. Close the zip half way at the bag top. Tack both sides of the zip together at the opened end of the bag top so it sits evenly. Turn the bag inside out.

12. Open up the raw section of the bag top corner at the closed zip end and re-arrange this so that the bag side seam and the zip (bag top) are now on top of each other, right sides together. Accessing through the inside, insert one of the ring holders (with ring) into the gap, sandwiching the raw edge of the ring holder between the bag side and the bag zip. Ensure that all raw edges are positioned evenly on top of each other. Sew the layers together along the raw edge, capturing the ring holder in the process. Trim away the excess zip. Repeat with the remaining top corner of the bag and ring holder then turn the bag right side out.

13. Place one of the 47 x 3.5cm (18½ x 1⅜in) adjustable strap lengths right sides together with the bag back so the raw edges meet. Position the strap 9.5cm (3¾in) from one side of the back centre seams and tack in place. Repeat with the remaining strap to the other side of the seam, as shown.

6
Zip
Tacking (basting)

13 Bag back
Adjustable strap
Tacking

14. Fully open the zip and turn the main bag inside out again. Mark the quarter points on the interfaced bag base piece and the main bottom raw edge. Ensuring that the straps stay within the bag, tack the bag base into position along the bottom raw edge of the bag, right sides together, matching up the quarter points. Position the base so the bag seams will become centre bag front and centre bag back. When you are happy with the fit, tack and then sew the base into place. Turn the bag right side out.

When positioning the bag base you will find it easier to pin the quarter points first before easing the remaining sections in place.

15. Take the main bag lining pieces and fold the top edge only under by 5mm (¼in). Press well. Place the two lining pieces on top of each other, right sides together, and sew together along the two side edges only. Insert the bag base in the bottom of the lining (see Step 14).

16. With the lining bag inside out, fold the raw top corners, as shown. Sew together along the raw edges.

17. Keeping the main bag right side out and the lining bag right side in, place the lining bag inside the main bag. Neatly and evenly pin the folded under edge at the lining opening around the inside of the zip. Ladder stitch the lining in place all the way around the zip (see Useful Stitches).

18. Take one of the remaining shoulder strap pieces and thread one end through the ring at the bag front. Fold the strap under onto itself by approximately 2.5cm (1in), enclosing the ring. Topstitch in place. Repeat with the other shoulder strap.

19. In the same way, thread the other end of one of the shoulder straps around the top bar of one of the adjustable straps. Fold under by 2.5cm (1in) and topstitch in place. Repeat with the other shoulder strap.

20. Take the ends of the shoulder straps with the adjusters attached and insert them through the ring at the bag back and to the back of the bag. Attach the loose ends of the straps from the bottom of the bag through the strap adjusters and adjust to the desired length (see Adjustable Straps).

16 Lining bag (inside out)

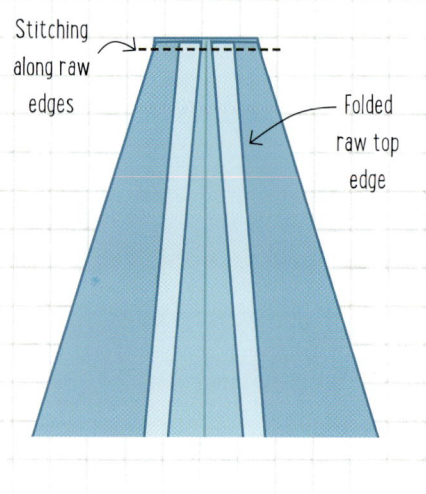

Stitching along raw edges

Folded raw top edge

BLUE SKIES BACKPACK

MELLY'S MESSENGER

This trendy messenger bag is super practical for everyday use and will comfortably fit a good supply of paper and books. Inside there is a large double pocket as well as an internal divider to keep everything organized and easy to find. This simple design can be made as bright and fun or as minimalistic as you like – it will look classic in any combination.

SKILL RATING:

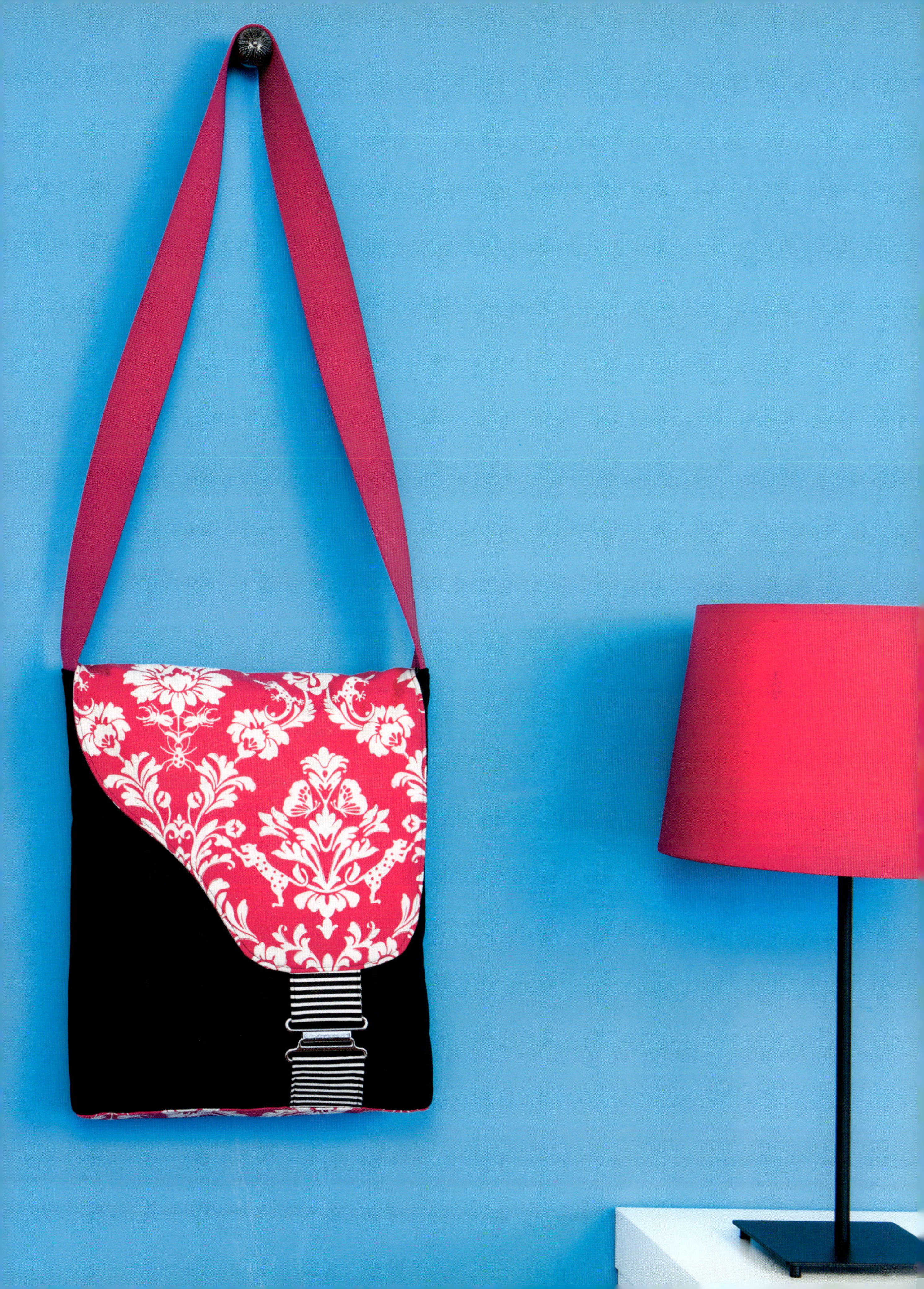

You will need

- 61cm (24in) black home décor weight fabric for main bag and internal divider
- 38cm (15in) pink print home décor weight fabric for bag flap, base and pocket
- 40cm (15¾in) black and white stripe patchwork fabric for lining and buckle holder
- 1m (40in) lightweight fusible fleece
- 15cm (6in) square lightweight woven fusible interfacing
- 1.1m (44in) of 4.5cm (1¾in) wide cotton strap webbing
- Silver cummerbund buckle (Birch brand)

Finished size: 37 x 29cm (14½ x 11½in) excluding handle

MELLY'S MESSENGER

Cutting

1. Trace all of the Melly's Messenger templates (see Pattern Pullout Sheet) onto tracing paper or template plastic, transferring all the markings and cutting them out around the traced lines.

2. From the black home décor weight fabric, cut two pieces measuring 35.5 x 39.5cm (14¼ x 15½in) for the main bag and two pieces measuring 30 x 29cm (12 x 11½in) for the internal divider.

3. From the pink print home décor weight fabric, trace the bag flap template once onto the folded fabric and cut out along the traced line to make two pieces. Next cut a strip measuring 36 x 7.5cm (14¼ x 3in) for the bag base and another piece measuring 28cm (11in) square for the internal pocket.

4. From the black and white stripe patchwork fabric, cut two 36 x 39.5cm (14¼ x 15½in) pieces for the lining and one piece measuring 28cm (11in) square for the internal pocket lining. Now cut two pieces measuring 12.5 x 7cm (5 x 2¾in) for the bottom buckle holder and two pieces measuring 10 x 7cm (4 x 2¾in) for the flap buckle holder.

5. From the lightweight fusible fleece, cut four pieces measuring 35.5 x 39.5cm (14¼ x 15½in) for the main bag and lining. Trace the bag flap template once and cut out along the traced lines. Next cut out the 30 x 29cm (12 x 11½in) internal divider, a 35.5 x 5cm (14 x 2in) strip, and a piece measuring 28cm (11in) square for the internal pocket.

6. From the lightweight woven fusible interfacing, cut one piece measuring 7 x 12.5cm (2¾ x 5in) for the bottom buckle holder and one piece measuring 7 x 10cm (2¾ x 4in) for the flap buckle holder.

Preparation

1. Interface the main bag pieces, the lining pieces, half of the bag flap, the pocket and the divider pieces with the matching lightweight fusible fleece pieces.

2. Interface one each of the flap buckle and bottom buckle pieces with lightweight woven fusible interfacing.

Construction

5mm (¼in) seam allowance included.

1. Place the two black main bag pieces on top of each other, right sides together. Sew together along the bottom 35.5cm (14in) edge and press the seams open.

2. Iron the 35.5 x 5cm (14 x 2in) piece of fusible fleece to the centre of the 35.5 x 7.5cm (14 x 3in) pink fabric panel, so you have 1.5cm (½in) of fabric on either side of the fleece. Fold the extra 1.5cm (½in) of fabric under along both sides and press well in place to form the bag base panel.

3. Place the two bottom buckle pieces on top of each other, right sides together. Sew together along both 12.5cm (5in) edges, turn and press. Thread through the female section of the cummerbund buckle and fold onto itself to create a loop. Tack (baste) the raw edges together, enclosing the buckle (see Useful Stitches).

4. Open out the main bag from Step 1 and lay it out, right side up, so the bottom seam is flat on the work surface. Centre the base panel, right side up, over the seam so 2.5cm (1in) of the base is placed over the bag front and 2.5cm (1in) is placed over the bag back. Make sure that the folded under 1.5cm (½in) on each side of the base panel remains underneath. Now position the bottom buckle piece so that the raw edge sits under the base panel by 1cm (⅜in) and the buckle piece is positioned 9cm (3½in) in from the right bag edge. Pin everything in place then topstitch onto the bag along both edges, as shown (see Useful Stitches).

5. Place the main bag right sides together again so that both the top edges and side edges meet evenly. Sew the bag sides together all the way from the top to the bottom.

6. Keeping the bag inside out, follow the box corner technique (see Box Corners), sewing across where the triangle measures 5cm (2in) (from one edge of the base panel to the other). Repeat for the other corner. Trim the excess fabric approximately 1.5cm (½in) outside of the sewn line.

The box corners will be very thick, so take care with your needle and sew over the stitching a few times for added strength.

4 Main bag piece (opened out)

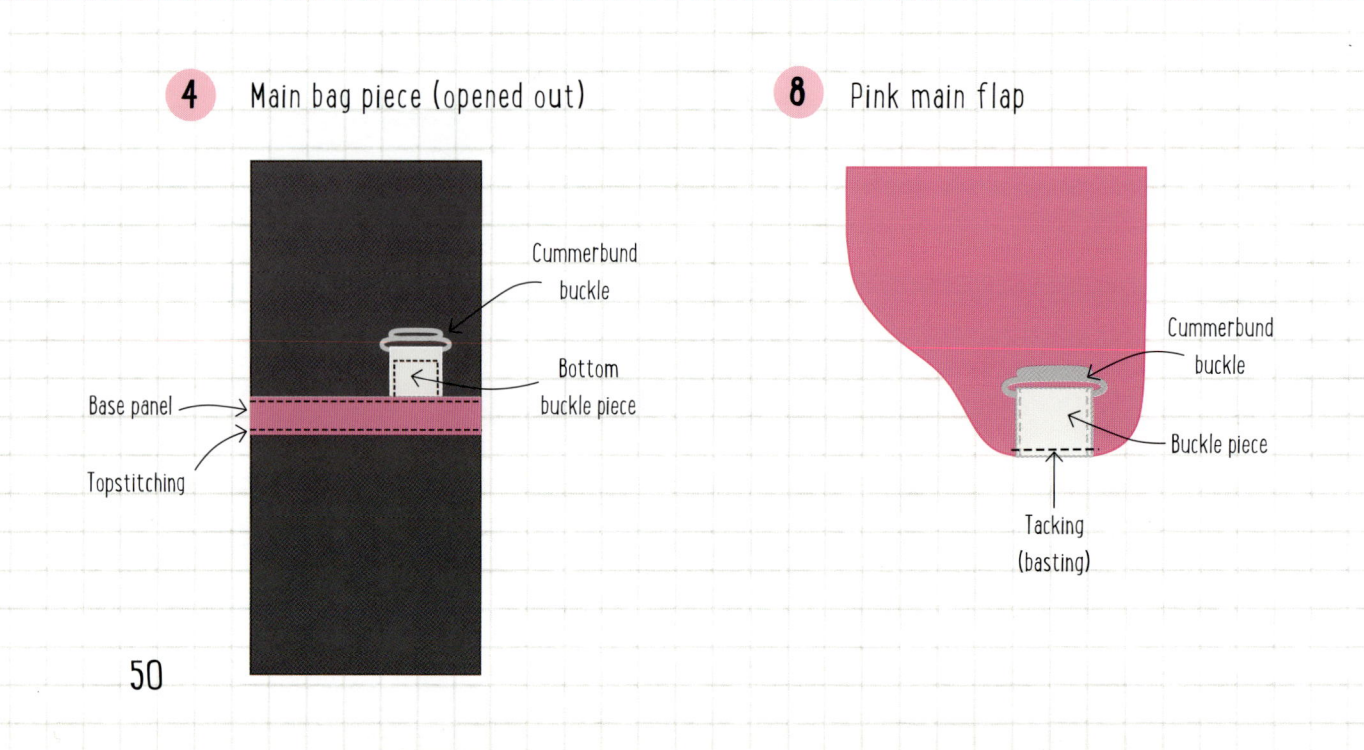

- Base panel
- Topstitching
- Cummerbund buckle
- Bottom buckle piece

8 Pink main flap

- Cummerbund buckle
- Buckle piece
- Tacking (basting)

MELLY'S MESSENGER

7. Place the two flap buckle pieces on top of each other, right sides together. Sew together along both 10cm (4in) edges, then turn and press. Topstitch the strip along both 10cm (4in) edges. Thread this strip through the male section of the cummerbund buckle and fold it onto itself to create a loop. Tack the raw edges together, enclosing the buckle.

8. Position the buckle piece onto the pink main flap piece, right sides together, as shown. The raw edges should meet and the buckle piece should be centred, following the marking on the flap template. Tack into place.

9. Place the two bag flap pieces on top of each other, right sides together. Sew together along the side and bottom edges, leaving the top straight edge open for turning. Turn and press well. Topstitch the flap along the sewn edges and machine tack the straight top edges together.

10. Place the bag flap on top of the bag back, right sides together, ensuring that the flap is evenly centred along the width. Tack into place along the top raw edges, as shown.

11. Trim the strap webbing to the desired length. Centre each end of the handle strap over either side seam on the main bag, right sides together, and tack in place. Put the main bag aside.

The bag handle can be shortened to suit the height of the wearer. I used the full 1.1m (44in) length, however, I am very tall!

12. Place the two pocket pieces on top of each other, right sides together. Sew together along all four edges, leaving a 7.5cm (3in) gap in one side for turning. Snip the corners, turn and press well. Topstitch along the pocket top edge with a double row of stitching.

13. Place one of the bag lining pieces right side up on your work surface. Position the pocket onto the lining piece, approximately 7.5cm (3in) down from the top raw edge. Ensuring that the pocket is centred within the width, pin then sew in place along the side and bottom edges. Sew a line of stitching from the centre top to the centre bottom to create a double pocket, if desired.

14. Place the two divider pieces on top of each other, right sides together. Sew together along both 30cm (12in) edges, turn right side out and press well. Topstitch along both 30cm (12in) edges with a double row of stitching.

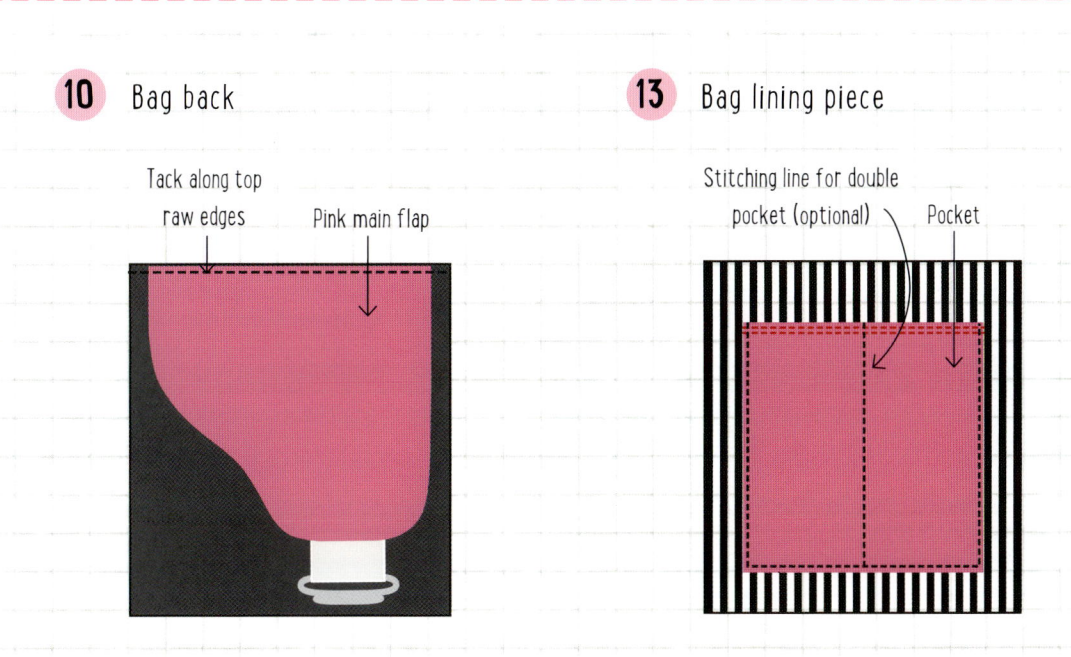

10 Bag back
- Tack along top raw edges
- Pink main flap

13 Bag lining piece
- Stitching line for double pocket (optional)
- Pocket

15. Place the lining front and back pieces on top of each other, right sides together. Place the divider in-between these two layers to create a sandwich. One of the raw divider side edges needs to sit against the raw left-hand side edges of the lining pieces, 4.5cm (1¾in) up from the bottom lining edge.

16. Sew the left-hand side edges of the lining pieces together, capturing the divider edge in your sewing. Sew the bottom edge of the lining pieces together, leaving an 18cm (7in) gap in the centre for turning. Now position the remaining raw edge of the divider along the raw right-hand side edges of the bag lining. The divider is narrower than the lining, so pin or tack it evenly in place to secure, ensuring it is also 4.5cm (1¾in) up from the bottom lining edge. Next sew the right-hand side of the lining pieces together.

17. Keeping the lining bag inside out, follow the box corner technique (see Box Corners), sewing across where the triangle measures 5cm (2in). Repeat for the other corner. Trim the excess fabric approximately 5mm (¼in) outside the sewn line.

18. Keeping the main bag right side out and the bag lining right side in, place the main bag inside the lining bag. Push the handle strap and closure flap inside between the two layers, making sure that they are well clear of the top edge, and then pin evenly all the way around the top edge. Now carefully sew all the way around the top of the bag. Turn the bag right side out through the hole in the bottom of the lining and push the lining inside the main bag. Topstitch the top bag edge. Finally, ladder stitch the turning gap closed (see Useful Stitches).

TRY THIS!

Melly's Messenger would make a fabulously sturdy children's book bag. Simply shorten the strap to suit the childs frame.

The cummerbund buckle should be readily available online. If you have trouble finding one, simply use magnetic closures on the flap and omit the buckle holders.

MELLY'S MESSENGER

HAPPY HOBO BAG

This fresh and fashionable hobo bag is so quick and easy to put together, it's perfect for beginners. With a handy little print pocket on the front for quick access items and plenty of room inside for all your everyday needs, it is practical and comfortable on the shoulder, yet still entirely fun and playful. This cute and colourful design is sure to bring a smile to your face!

SKILL RATING:

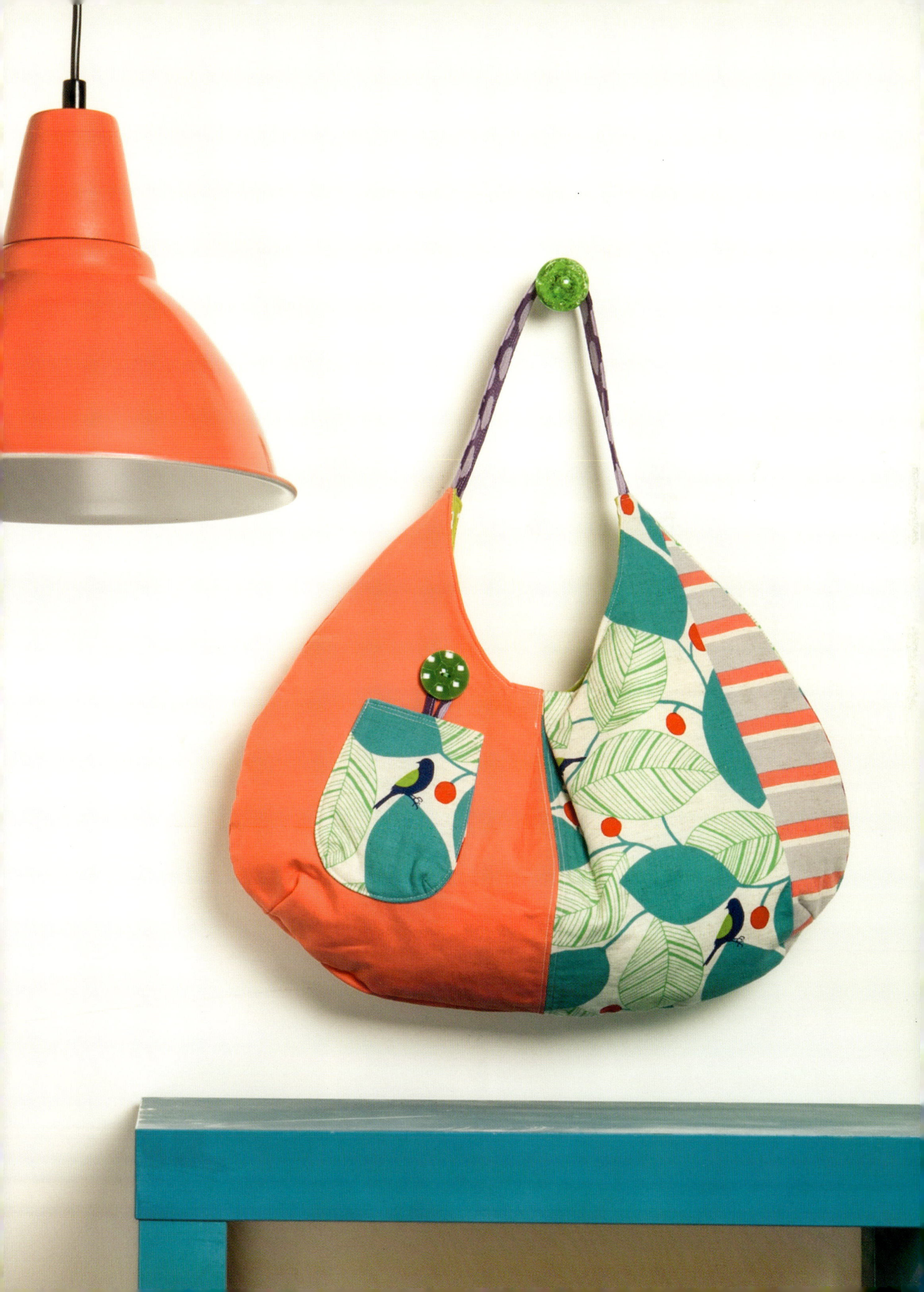

You will need

- Patterned print fabric (any weight) for the main bag: 40.5cm (16in) if your print is directional like mine; if not use 28cm (11in)
- 28cm (11in) solid coral fabric (any weight) for bag panels
- 5cm (2in) purple co-ordinating print for handle and pocket closure
- 40.5cm (16in) green lining fabric
- 55cm (22in) lightweight fusible fleece
- 3cm (1¼in) sturdy matching button
- Magnetic closure

Finished size: 50 x 43cm (20 x 17in) including handles

HAPPY HOBO BAG

Cutting

1. Trace all of the Happy Hobo Bag templates (see Pattern Pullout Sheet) onto tracing paper or template plastic, transferring all the markings and cutting them out around the traced lines.

2. From the main patterned print fabric, cut two 40.5 x 28cm (16 x 11in) panels for the main outer bag. Now trace the pocket template once onto the folded remaining fabric and cut out along the traced line to form two pieces.

3. From the solid coral fabric, cut two 40.5 x 28cm (16 x 11in) panels for the main outer bag.

4. From the purple fabric, cut two 38 x 5cm (15 x 2in) strips for the handle. Now cut two 16.5 x 2.5cm (6½ x 1in) strips for the pocket closure.

5. From the green lining fabric, trace the main bag template twice and cut out along the traced lines.

6. From the lightweight fusible fleece, trace the main bag template twice and cut out along the traced lines. Cut out the rectangle at the centre top of each piece, following the dashed line marking on the template. Now cut one strip measuring 38 x 5cm (15 x 2in) for the handle. Trace the pocket template once and cut out along the traced lines.

Preparation

1. Interface one of the pocket and one of the handle strip pieces with the matching lightweight fusible fleece pieces.

TRY THIS!
If you prefer a longer handled bag, simply adjust the lengths of your handle and fusible fleece strips to suit your preference.

Construction

5mm (¼in) seam allowance included.

1. Place one of the patterned and one of the coral main bag panels on top of each other, right sides together. Sew them together along one 40.5cm (16in) edge. Press the seam open. Repeat with the remaining main bag panels to create a mirror image piece.

2. Ensuring that the line down the centre of the template is evenly placed on the seam of the panels, trace the main bag template onto both panels created in Step 1 and cut out along the traced lines. Interface both main bag pieces with matching lightweight fusible fleece. Now topstitch both edges of the seam down the bag front and back.

3. To create the pleats at the centre top of the bag front, fold the points marked with a star on the template inwards, so that they meet the centre seam at the bag top edge. Topstitch the pleats into place with a 4cm (1½in) line of sewing (see Useful Stitches), as shown. Repeat for the bag back.

4. Sew the darts together (see Sewing Darts), as marked at the bottom of the bag front and back pieces.

5. Repeat Steps 3 and 4 with the bag lining pieces.

6. Take the pocket closure strip, fold one short end in by approximately 5mm (¼in) and press. Fold the strip in half, right side out, all the way along the length. Press the fold in place and reopen. Now fold the raw edges evenly into the centre fold and press again. Refold the entire strip to hide the raw edges, press then topstitch down the strip to secure.

You could also substitute this fabric closure tie with a length of fine cord or trim – just make sure that it's tough enough to endure the traffic and thin enough to be able to wrap behind a button.

7. Sew the darts into place on both of the pocket pieces (see Sewing Darts).

8. Place the pocket front and the closure strip on top of each other, right sides together, so that the raw edges meet at the centre top of the pocket. Tack (baste) into place (see Useful Stitches), as shown.

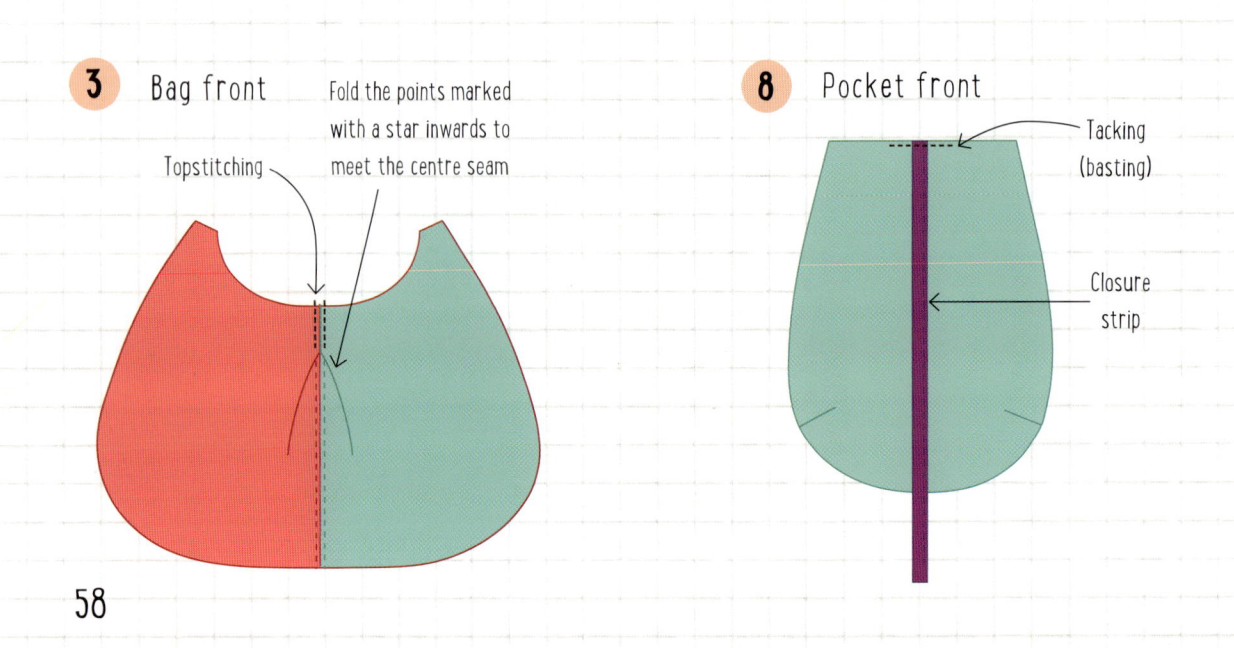

3 Bag front — Fold the points marked with a star inwards to meet the centre seam
Topstitching

8 Pocket front — Tacking (basting), Closure strip

HAPPY HOBO BAG

9. Place the two pocket pieces on top of each other, right sides together. Sew together along all edges, leaving a 5cm (2in) gap in one side edge for turning, and ensuring that the loose end of the closure strip is not accidentally captured in your sewing. Snip the top pocket corners and turn right side out. Press and topstitch the pocket along the top edge with a double row of stitches.

10. Place the pocket onto the bag front, right side up, referring to the photo as a guide for placement. Topstitch the pocket into place, close to the edge along the side and bottom edges.

11. Sew the button approximately 1.5–2cm (½–¾in) above the pocket top, tightly and securely as the closure strip will be tightly wound around it.

12. Place the bag front and back on top of each other, right sides together. Ensuring that the centre and dart seams meet, sew the bag pieces together all the way along the side and bottom curved edges only. Turn right side out. Repeat to sew together the two lining pieces, leaving a 22.5cm (9in) gap in the centre bottom edge for turning, but do not turn.

13. Keeping the main bag right side out and the lining bag right side in, place the main bag inside the lining bag. Tack the main bag and lining together all the way along the top curved edges only and sew into place. You will have a small remaining unsewn angled section at both bag top corners, which will be used to insert the handle. Do not turn right side out. Snip the seam allowance along the curved edge.

14. Place the two handle strips on top of each other, right sides together. Sew together, leaving one short end open for turning and turn right side out (see Turning Handles). Snip the sewn end off and press well. Referring to the photograph, topstitch the handle every 3mm (⅛in) along the length.

15. With the bag still remaining inside out, open and rearrange the raw edges at one of the unsewn open top corners, so that the main bag fabric is now on top of the lining fabric. Insert one end of the handle strip in through the turning gap of the lining and position it to meet the raw edge between the main bag and the lining. The raw edge of the handle strip should meet the raw edge of the fabric. Sew in place.

16. Take the remaining loose end of the handle strip and, again accessing through the gap in the lining, insert this into the other open top bag corner. Sew together in the same manner. Snip the corners and turn the bag right side out. Topstitch all the way along the top edge of the bag.

17. Insert the magnetic closure into the centre of the lining, approximately 1.5cm (½in) down from the top edge (see Inserting Magnetic Closures). Finally, slipstitch the opening in the lining closed.

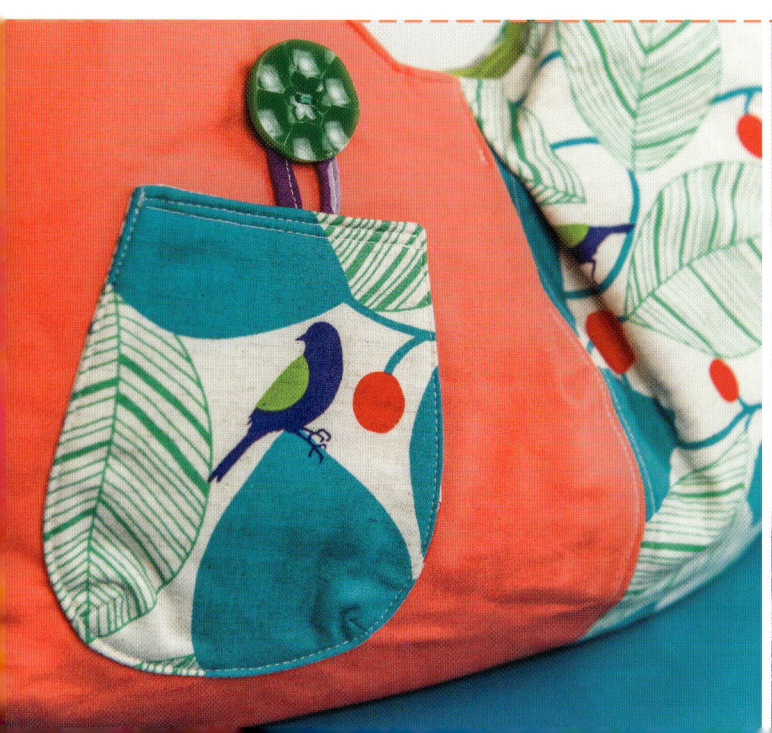

MOBILE MUMMY CHANGING BAG

When there are little ones in your life, it seems as if you need to carry everything! This smart changing bag with its cute cherry print detail is ideal for fitting in all those baby necessities. There are internal and external pockets for all the little essentials, such as soothers, rattles and snacks, plus a matching machine-washable changing mat to make change times a breeze. The generous strap can be adjusted to fit either over your shoulder or the pram.

SKILL RATING:

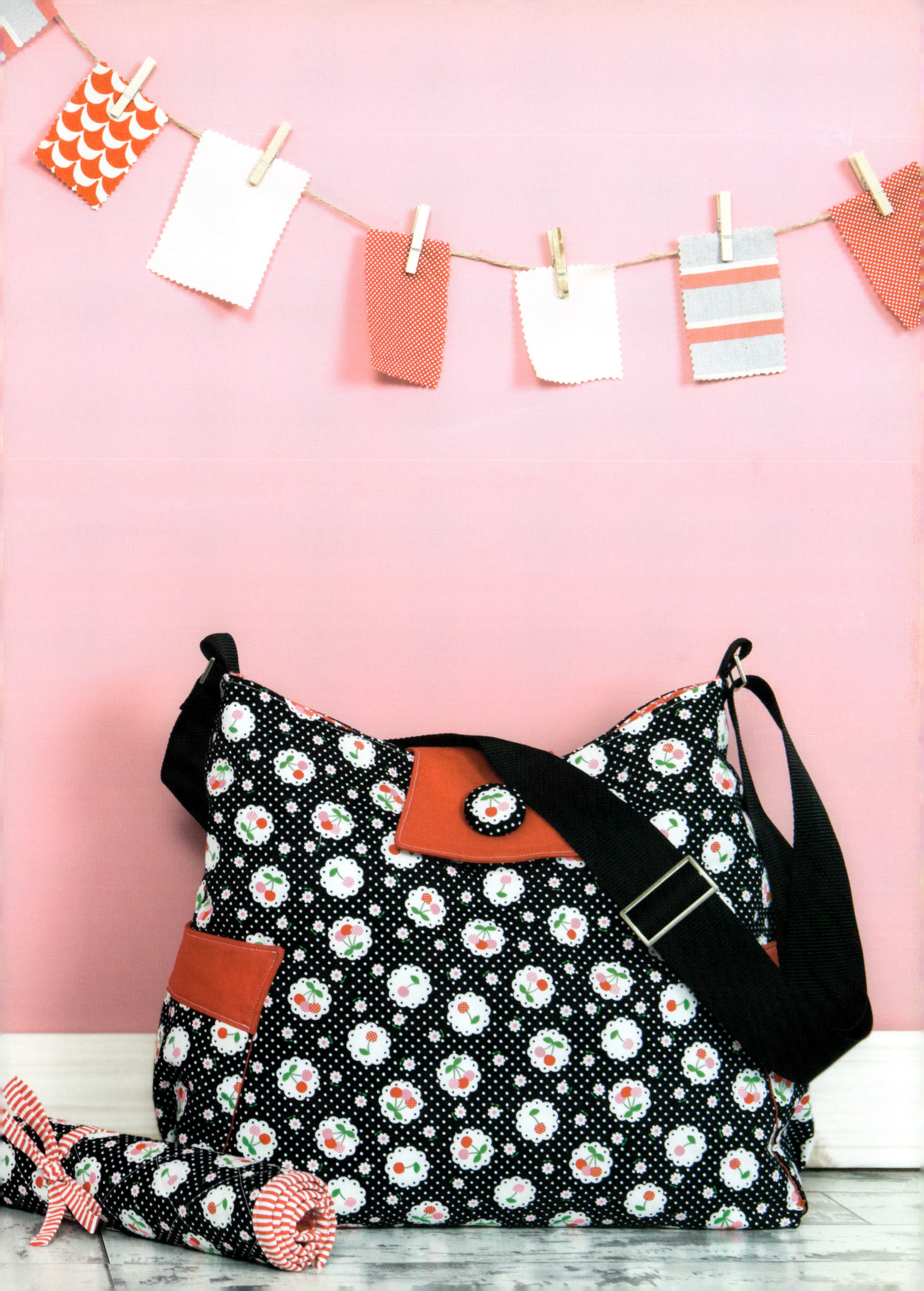

You will need

- 91.5cm (36in) home décor weight non-directional print fabric for main bag and mat (for a directional print, you will need approximately 38cm (15in) more)
- 91.5cm (36in) red non-directional print lining fabric (any weight)
- 55cm (22in) solid red linen/cotton blend fabric for internal pockets and trims
- 1.4m (1½yd) lightweight fusible fleece
- 53.5 x 33cm (21 x 13in) thin wadding (batting) for changing mat
- 1.65m (1⅞yd) of 5cm (2in) wide black webbing for strap
- Two 5cm (2in) oblong rings
- 5cm (2in) oblong slide adjuster
- Large decorative button (I used a self-cover button)
- 2m (2¼yd) of 2.5cm (1in) wide bias tape, or enough fabric to make this for the changing mat
- 10cm (4in) hook and loop tape

Finished size: Changing Bag: 36 x 43cm (14¼ x 17in) including handle
Changing Mat: 53.5 x 33cm (21 x 13in)

MOBILE MUMMY CHANGING BAG

Cutting

1. Trace all of the Mobile Mummy Changing Bag templates (see Pattern Pullout Sheet) onto tracing paper or template plastic, transferring all the markings and cutting them out around the traced lines.

2. From the home décor weight print fabric, cut two 16.5 x 23cm (6½ x 9in) pieces for the external pockets. Trace the main bag template twice onto the remaining fabric and cut out along the traced lines. Cut one panel measuring 52.5 x 32.5cm (21 x 13in) for the changing mat.

3. From the red non-directional print lining fabric, cut one panel measuring 53.5 x 33cm (21 x 13in) for the changing mat. Trace the main bag template twice onto the remaining fabric and cut out along the traced lines.

4. From the solid red linen/ cotton blend fabric, cut two strips measuring 23 x 7.5cm (9 x 3in). Next cut four panels measuring 34.5 x 25cm (13½ x 10in) for the internal pockets. Trace the pocket template and the closure flap template twice and cut out along the traced lines.

5. From the lightweight fusible fleece, trace the main bag template four times and cut out along the traced lines. Now cut two panels measuring 34.5 x 25cm (13½ x 10in) for the internal pockets. Trace the closure flap template once and the pocket template twice and cut out along the traced lines.

Preparation

1. Interface the main bag pieces, main bag lining pieces, two internal pocket pieces and one closure flap piece with matching lightweight fusible fleece pieces.

2. If you are using a self-ßcover button, interface a decorative cut scrap of the main bag fabric with fusible fleece and use to cover the button, following the manufacturer's instructions.

When tracing the main bag template twice onto fabric you will need to position the template sideways in order to fit two within the width.

Construction

5mm (¼in) seam allowance included.

CHANGING BAG

1. Place one of the 16.5 x 23.5cm (6½ x 9in) external pocket pieces on top of one of the 23.5 x 7.5cm (9 x 3in) red fabric strips, with right sides together. Sew together along one 23.5cm (9in) edge and press. Trace the pocket template (see Pattern Pullout Sheet) onto this, so that the marked line meets the seam in the fabric. Cut out along the traced line then interface with one of the matching pieces of fusible fleece. Topstitch the seam along the red fabric seam of the pocket. Repeat to create the second pocket front.

2. Place one of the pocket pieces created in Step 1 on top of one of the red pocket lining pieces, with right sides together. Sew the pocket together by stitching along the side and top edges only. Snip the corners, turn and press, then topstitch the pocket along the top curved edge. Repeat to create the second pocket.

3. Take one of your pockets and following the markings on the pocket template piece (see Pattern Pullout Sheet), fold both layers of fabric from the centre markings out to meet the outer markings. This will create two pleats, as shown in the photograph. Tack (baste) the pleats in place along the raw edge (see Useful Stitches). Repeat for the second pocket.

4. Centre the 'loop' half of the hook and loop tape length onto one of the main bag pieces, 6cm (2½in) down from the top raw edge. Topstitch into place (see Useful Stitches), as shown, to create the bag front.

5. Place the two main bag pieces on top of each other, right sides together. Sew them together along one side edge only and press. Place this on your work surface, right side up, and then centre one of your pockets over the seam, as shown. Ensuring that the bottom raw edge of the pocket meets the raw edge of the bag, topstitch the pocket along the side edges onto the main bag.

6. Place the main bag pieces right sides together again, then sew the remaining side edges of the bag together. Position the remaining pocket onto this side seam and sew onto the bag as in Step 5.

7. Position the bag front and back on top of each other evenly again, then sew the bottom edge only together. You will have a remaining unsewn angled section between the bag sides and bottom.

4 One main bag piece

'Loop' half of hook and loop tape length

Topstitching

MOBILE MUMMY CHANGING BAG

8. Sew the bottom box corners together (see Box Corners), capturing the bottom edge of the pockets in the process.

9. Take one of the interfaced and one of the non-interfaced internal pocket pieces and place them on top of each other, right sides together. Sew together along all four edges, leaving a 10cm (4in) gap in the centre bottom for turning. Snip the corners, turn and press. Topstitch the top 33cm (13in) edge with a double row of topstitching. Repeat to create the second pocket piece.

10. Take one of the bag lining pieces, right sides up, and place the pocket centrally on top of this, also right side up. Position the pocket approximately 7.5cm (3in) from the top lining edge and topstitch in place along the side and bottom edges only to create a large internal pocket. Repeat with the second bag lining piece and internal pocket, this time

Feel free to add extra rows of topstitching to one or both of your pockets to create custom-sized sections for those smaller often-used items.

adding another row of topstitching from the centre top to the centre bottom to create a double pocket, as shown.

11. Place the two bag lining pieces on top of each other, right sides together. Sew the lining front and lining back together along the side and bottom edges, this time leaving a 20cm (8in) gap in the centre of the bottom edge for turning. Now sew in the box corners as you did for the main bag in Step 8.

12. Thread a 7.5cm (3in) length of black webbing through one of the oblong handle rings. Fold the webbing onto itself and tack (baste) the raw edges together, securing the ring. Position the ring holder on top of one of the main bag side seams, so that the raw tacked (basted) edge of the webbing meets the top raw edge of the bag side. Tack (baste) into place. Repeat to create the ring holder on the other side of the bag.

13. Keeping the main bag right side out and the lining bag right side in, place the main bag inside the lining bag. Sew the main bag and lining together all the way along the top edges. Turn right side out and ladder stitch the opening in the lining closed (see Useful Stitches).

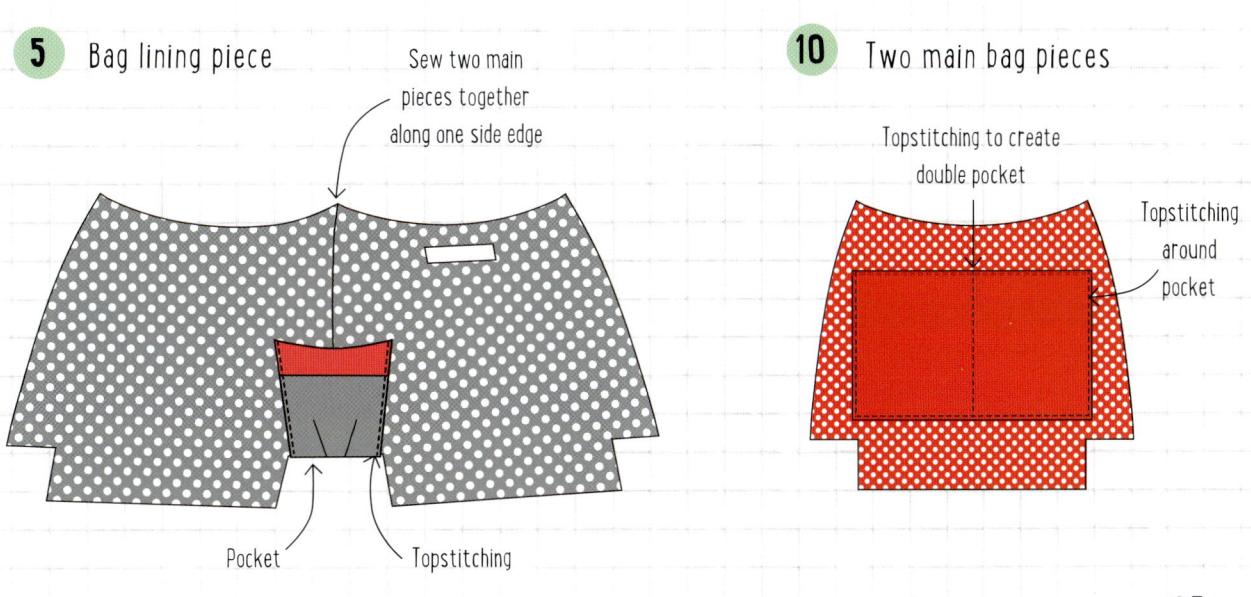

5 Bag lining piece

Sew two main pieces together along one side edge

Pocket   Topstitching

10 Two main bag pieces

Topstitching to create double pocket

Topstitching around pocket

14. Centre the 'hook' section of the hook and loop tape on top of the non-interfaced bag closure piece, 2.5cm (1in) from one straight edge Topstitch in place, as shown.

When sewing the back section of the closure flap in place, make sure that the lining is sitting flatly and neatly underneath to avoid messy or puckered lining.

15. Place the two bag closure pieces on top of each other, right sides together. Sew together along all edges, leaving a 5cm (2in) gap along one edge for turning. Snip the corners, turn and press, then topstitch along all edges. Attach the closure flap edges to the bag front with the hook and loop tape. Fold the other side over to the bag back and pin in place where desired. Topstitch the back section of the closure flap to the bag back.

16. Take a 1.5m (1½yd) length of black webbing, attach one end of the strap to the slide adjuster (see Adjustable Straps) then attach to the two oblong rings. To finish the raw ends of the webbing, simply fold under the raw edge and topstitch in place, as shown in the photograph.

17. Sew the covered button to the front of the closure flap as desired. This is purely decorative.

CHANGING MAT

18. Take the two pieces of remaining fabric for the changing mat. Make a sandwich with the outer fabric, wadding (batting) and internal fabric, so that both pieces of fabric are rights sides out. Pin well, then quilt the three layers together as desired. I quilted mine with a 5cm (2in) diagonal grid.

19. Take two 33cm (13in) lengths of bias tape, open up one end and fold the raw edge in. Refold the bias tape, fold the strip in half along the entire length, right sides out, and press well. Topstitch the bias tape in this folded position to create one tie and repeat to create a second tie. Place the two ties on top of each other so that the raw ends meet and tack (baste) the raw ends together. Place the ties onto the outer side of the changing mat so that the raw edges meet the centre top raw edge of the quilted mat and tack (baste) in place.

20. Take the remaining length of bias tape, fold along the entire length, right sides out, and press. Use this length of bias tape to bind the changing mat (see Topstitch Binding), mitring the corners as you go (see Mitring Corners).

21. To finish, roll up the changing mat and secure in place with a bow using the two ties.

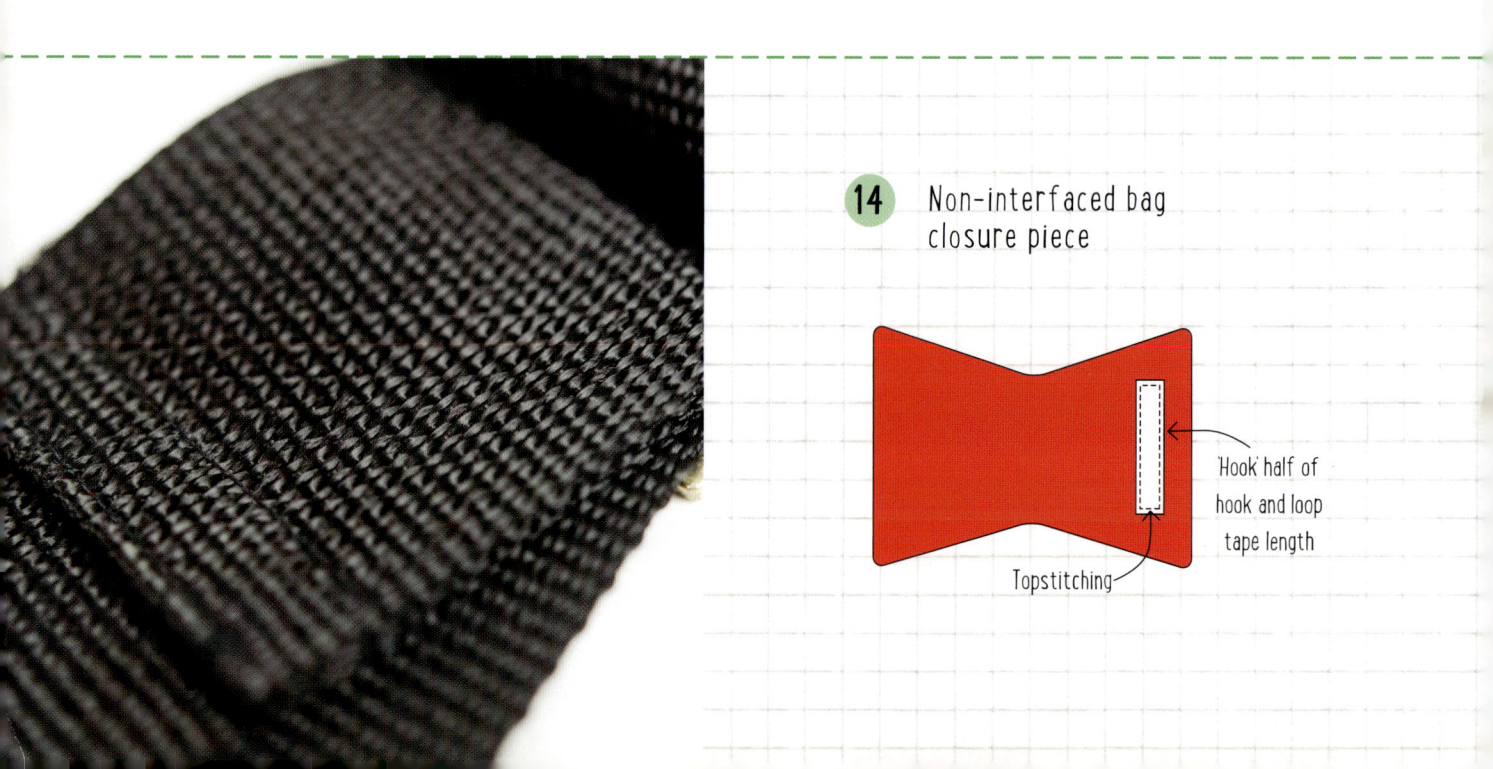

14 Non-interfaced bag closure piece

'Hook' half of hook and loop tape length

Topstitching

MOBILE MUMMY CHANGING BAG

SHOPAHOLIC'S SHOPPER

The true shopaholic loves to go shopping in style, and this gorgeous bag is just the right accessory for her daily shopping needs – everything but the kitchen sink will fit inside! With its generous panelling and sturdy base, it is ideal for trips to the supermarket or farmers' market, and could even double up as the perfect beach bag or project bag!

SKILL RATING:

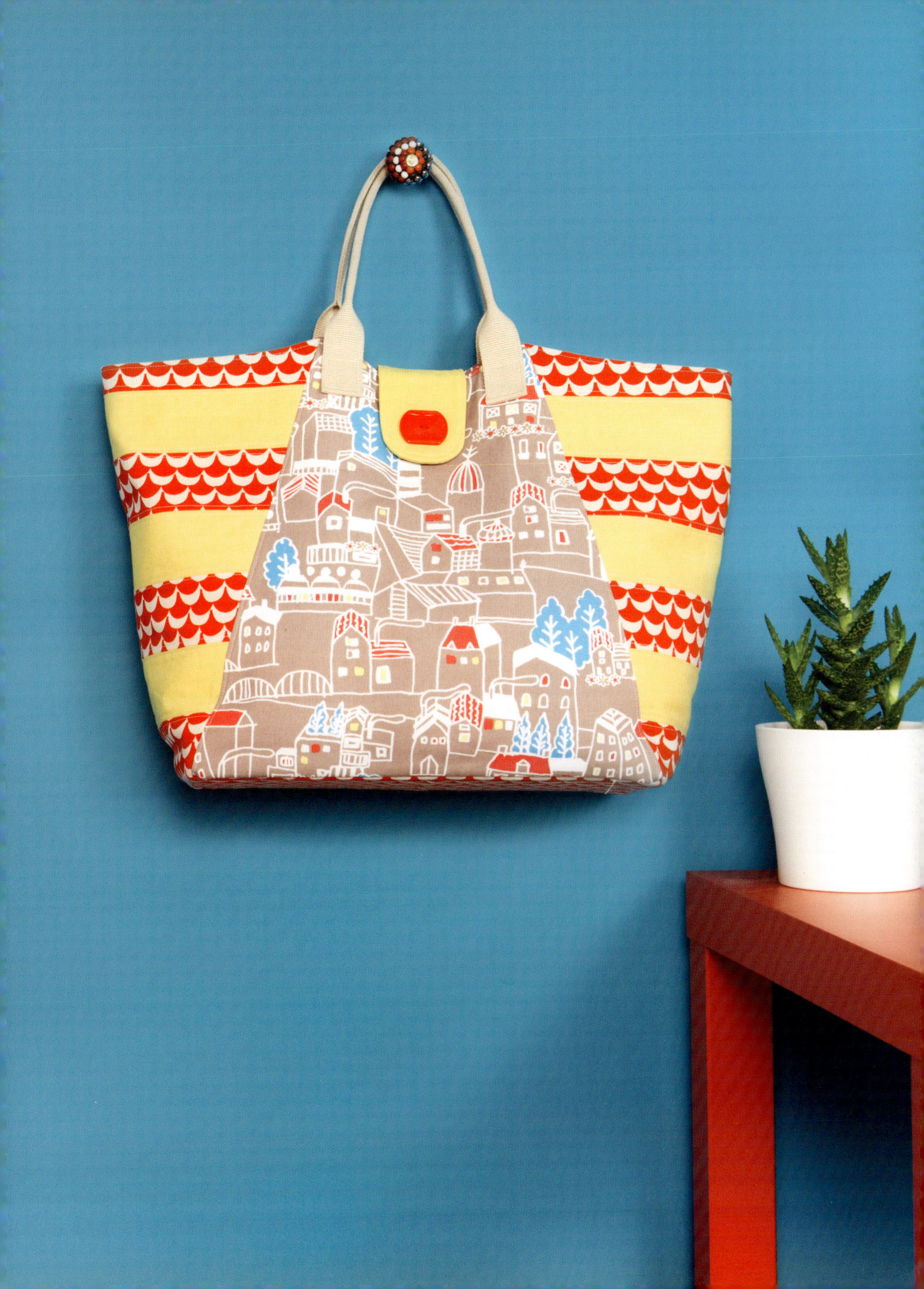

You will need

- 76cm (30in) taupe home décor weight fabric for central bag panels
- 36cm (14¼in) red scallop home décor weight fabric for striped panels and base
- 20cm (8in) green home décor weight fabric for striped panels
- 76cm (30in) lightweight fusible fleece
- 1m (40in) of 4cm (1½in) wide cotton strap webbing
- Magnetic closure
- Large red button
- 34 x 16cm (13¼ x 6¼in) piece of bag base, heavy cardboard or thick template plastic

Finished size: 43 x 30cm (17 x 12in) excluding handles

Shopaholic's Shopper

Cutting

1. Trace all of the Shopaholic's Shopper templates (see Pattern Pullout Sheet) onto tracing paper or template plastic, transferring all the markings and cutting them out around the traced lines.

2. From the taupe home décor weight fabric, trace the bag template A twice from the Pattern Pullout Sheet onto folded fabric and cut out along the traced lines to make four pieces. Next flip the bag template B upside down, trace it once onto the folded fabric and cut out along the traced lines to create two pieces.

3. From the red scallop home décor weight print, cut four strips measuring 76 x 6.5cm (30 x 2½in), two pieces measuring 35.5 x 18cm (14 x 7in) for the main bag and lining base, and a further two pieces measuring 18 x 5cm (7 x 2in).

4. From the green home décor weight fabric, cut three strips measuring 76 x 6.5cm (30 x 2½in) and one piece measuring 20 x 15cm (8 x 6in).

5. From the lightweight fusible fleece, trace bag template A once onto the folded fleece and cut out along the traced lines to make two pieces. Cut one panel measuring 76 x 37cm (30 x 14½in), one piece measuring 20 x 15cm (8 x 6in) and another piece measuring 35.5 x 18cm (14 x 7in).

Preparation

1. Interface two of the taupe A pieces, one of the red bag base pieces and the 20 x 15cm (8 x 6in) green panel with the matching lightweight fusible fleece pieces.

TRY THIS!

To make this project super quick and simple, leave out the stripy piecing of the side panels and substitute with another cute home décor weight fabric.

Construction

5mm (¼in) seam allowance included.

1. Sew all of the 76 x 6.5cm (30 x 2½in) red and green fabric strips together alternately along the 76cm (30in) lengths to create a striped panel, as shown.

For the neatest end result, always sew all the strips together in the same direction.

2. Press all of the seams open, then fuse the fusible fleece panel of the same size to the wrong side of the striped panel. Topstitch the panel along both sides of each seam (see Useful Stitches).

3. Fold the striped pieced panel in half, right sides together, ensuring that all seams and fabric are evenly on top of each other. Trace bag template B (see Pattern Pullout Sheet) onto the folded panel and cut out along the traced lines.

4. Place one of the taupe bag A pieces with fleece and one of the striped bag B pieces on top of each other, right sides together, so that one long side edge meets, as shown. Sew together along the straight side edge, finishing your sewing 5mm (¼in) from the bottom straight edge. Repeat with the remaining interfaced A and striped B pieces.

5. Take the two pieces created in Step 4 and sew together in the same way to create a panel, as shown. Topstitch the seams on the taupe fabric side, again stopping 5mm (¼in) before the bottom edge. Now sew the remaining raw edges together, press and topstitch to the taupe seam side in the same way.

6. Place the interfaced bag base piece right side down, then place the two 18 x 5cm (7 x 2in) strips of red fabric on top of it, right sides up. Using the diagram as a reference, position each 18cm (7in) strip approximately 5cm (2in) in from the ends of the bag base and machine tack (baste) them into position (see Useful Stitches). These will become holders for the bag base insert.

7. Place one of the long edges of the bag base, right side together, with the bottom edge of a taupe section on the main bag. The base will be approximately 5mm (¼in) longer on each side. Sew the edges together, stopping and starting 5mm (¼in) from each edge of the bag base, so that you stop right at the seams of the main bag. Repeat with the remaining long edge of the bag base and the remaining bottom edge of the opposite taupe main bag panel.

8. Now position together one of the short ends of the bag base with the applicable red bottom straight edge of the main bag. Pin in place and then sew together in the same way as for the long edges (see Step 5). Repeat with the remaining base and bag edge so that the base is now completely in place.

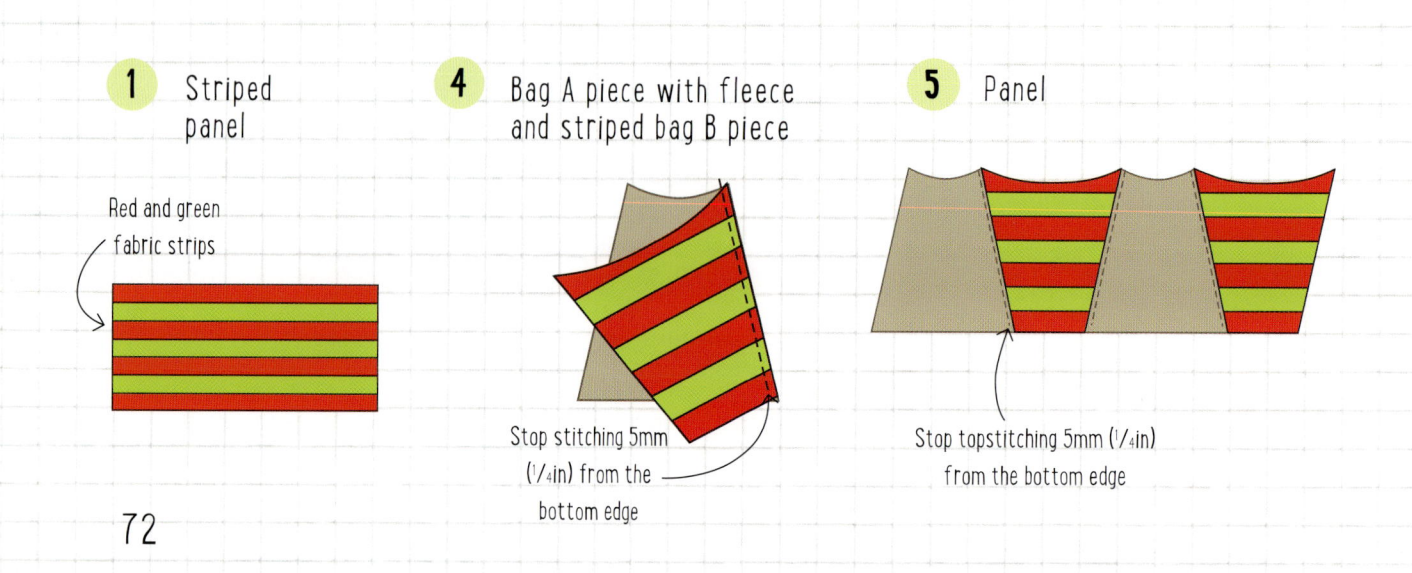

1 Striped panel

Red and green fabric strips

4 Bag A piece with fleece and striped bag B piece

Stop stitching 5mm (¼in) from the bottom edge

5 Panel

Stop topstitching 5mm (¼in) from the bottom edge

SHOPAHOLIC'S SHOPPER

9. Repeat Steps 4, 5, 7 and 8 with all of the bag lining pieces, this time leaving a 22.5cm (9in) gap in the centre of one of the long bag base seams for turning.

10. Fold the interfaced 20 x 15cm (8 x 6in) piece of green fabric in half, right sides together, so that it measures 10 x 15cm (4 x 6in). Trace the bag flap template (see Pattern Pullout Sheet) onto the wrong side and mark on the position for the magnetic closure and button. Insert the male side of the magnetic closure (see Inserting Magnetic Closures) into the right side at the marked position and then fold back, so that the fabric is folded right sides together again.

11. Sew along the traced line of the bag flap, leaving the top straight edge open for turning. Cut out the flap approximately 3–5mm (⅛–¼in) outside the sewn line. Turn and press well. Topstitch the bag flap along all sewn edges. Sew the button onto the right side of the flap at the same location as the magnetic closure beneath it.

12. Place the bag flap right sides together with the bag back. Machine tack (baste) the flap onto the centre, as shown.

13. Keeping the main bag right side out and the lining right side in, place the main bag inside the lining bag. Push the closure flap inside between the two layers so that it is clear of the top edge, then pin all the way around the top edge. Carefully sew all the way around the top of the bag. Snip the corners and turn the bag right side out through the gap in the bottom of the lining. Push the lining inside the main bag and topstitch the top bag edge.

14. Mark where the remaining female side of the magnetic closure should go, then insert it into the bag front, accessing this through the gap in the lining (see Inserting Magnetic Closures).

15. Now take the 34 x 16cm (13¼ x 6¼in) bag base insert. Carefully insert the base insert in through the turning gap, sliding it into the holders on the main bag base and adjusting, aligning and trimming it as required.

16. Cut two 50cm (20in) lengths of strap webbing. Fold the ends under on one piece by 2.5cm (1in) and press in place. Position the folded ends of the handle on top of the bag front so that they are just next to the seam, as shown in the photo below.

17. Topstitch the ends of the handle in place on the bag front. Now fold the loose section of the handle onto itself along the length and topstitch it in this folded position. Start and end the topstitching approximately 2.5cm (1in) from the top of the bag.

18. Repeat Steps 16–17 to create the back handle. Finally, ladder stitch the turning gap in the lining closed (see Useful Stitches).

The bag base insert adds base strength to the bag – you can use any thick and sturdy material.

6 Interfaced bag base piece
- Red fabric strips
- Machine tacking (basting)

12 Bag back
- Bag flap
- Machine tacking

SUGAR SWEET
SHOULDER BAG

This adorable shoulder bag has to be one of my favourite designs. With its pretty fabrics, floral button details and cute pastel colour scheme it has a real vintage feel, while doubling up as the perfect practical handbag for everyday use. The secure zipped-up main bag offers so much space and the easy access pockets on the front are handy for those small, often-used items. A bag that makes a bold statement!

SKILL RATING: 👜 👜 👜 👜

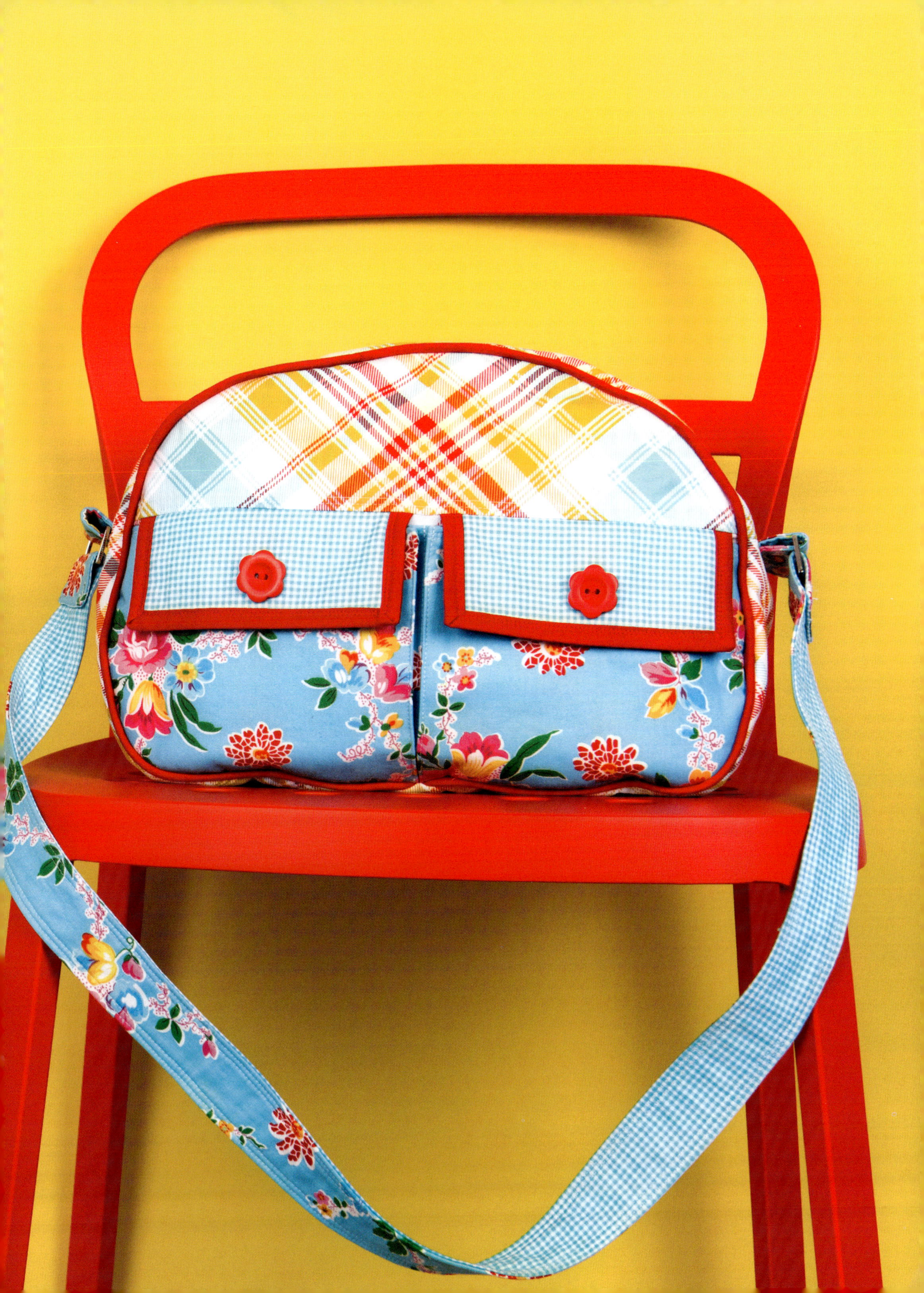

You will need

- 30cm (12in) diagonal check patchwork fabric for main bag and handle
- 40cm (15¾in) blue floral patchwork fabric for bag back, pockets and handle
- 45cm (17¾in) blue micro gingham patchwork fabric for lining and pocket flaps
- 1 fat quarter (18 x 22in) plain red patchwork fabric (or 2½m (2¾yd) premade red bias tape) for pocket flap binding
- 1m (40in) lightweight fusible fleece
- 2m (2¼yd) white cord to make piping
- Two magnetic closures
- Two medium red buttons
- Two 4cm (1½in) oblong rings
- One 46cm (18in) minimum red zip

Finished size: 22.5 x 31.5 x 11.5cm (9 x 12½ x 4½in) excluding handles

SUGAR SWEET SHOULDER BAG

Cutting

1. Trace all of the Sugar Sweet Shoulder Bag templates (see Pattern Pullout Sheet) onto tracing paper or template plastic, transferring all the markings and cutting them out around the traced lines.

2. From the diagonal check patchwork fabric, trace the bag top and bottom templates once and cut out along the traced lines. Cut one 54.5 x 12.5cm (21½ x 5in) strip and two 39.5 x 6.5cm (15½ x 2½in) strips.

3. From the blue floral patchwork fabric, trace the main bag template once and cut out along the traced line for the bag back. Cut two 40.5 x 16.5cm (16 x 6½in) pieces for the front pockets, one 1m x 5cm (40 x 2in) strip for the handle and two 15 x 5cm (6 x 2in) strips for the ring holders.

4. From the blue micro gingham patchwork fabric, trace the main bag template twice and cut out along the traced lines for the lining. Cut four 14 x 6.5cm (5½ x 2½in) pieces for the pocket flaps and one 1m x 5cm (40 x 2in) strip for the handle lining. Now cut one 54 x 12.5cm (21 x 5in) and two 39.5 x 6.5cm (15½ x 2½in) strips.

5. From the plain red patchwork fabric, cut two 30 x 4.5cm (12 x 1¾in) strips for the pocket flap binding and four 3cm (1¼in) strips on the bias, each measuring 56cm (22in) in length.

6. From the lightweight fusible fleece, trace the main bag template twice onto the folded fleece and cut out along the traced lines to make four pieces. Cut four 14 x 6.5cm (5½ x 2½in) pieces for the pocket flaps, one 15 x 5cm (6 x 2in) strip for the ring holders and one 1m x 5cm (40 x 2in) strip for the strap lining. Now cut two 54.5 x 12.5cm (21½ x 5in) strips, four 39.5 x 6cm (15½ x 2½in) strips and a 40.5 x 16.5cm (16 x 6½in) piece for the front pockets.

Preparation

1. Take the main bag piece, lining pieces, 12.5cm (5in) strips, 6.5cm (2½in) strips, pocket flap pieces, one of the front pocket pieces, one of the ring holder pieces and the main strap strip. Interface each piece with the matching lightweight fusible fleece pieces.

2. Create two 1m (40in) lengths of piping with the red fabric bias strips and white cord (see Creating Piping).

77

Construction

5mm (¼in) seam allowance included.

1. Place two of the pocket flap pieces on top of each other, right sides out. Tack (baste) the side and bottom edges together (see Useful Stitches), leaving the top straight edge open.

If you have a bias tape maker you could alternatively use this to make your pocket flap binding.

2. Fold a 30 x 4.5cm (12 x 1¾in) red patchwork binding strip in half along the length, right side out, and press. Fold the long raw edges into the fold and press again. Use this strip to bind the three tacked edges of the pocket flap (see Topstitch Binding). Mitre the corners as you go (see Mitre Topstitch Binding).

3. Now insert the male side of one of the magnetic closures into the lining side of the pocket flap (see Inserting Magnetic Closures). The closure should be centred within the width and approximately 2–2.5cm (¾–1in) up from the flap edge. Now sew a red button onto the front side of the flap in the same location as the closure, as shown in the photograph.

4. Repeat Steps 1–3 to create the second pocket flap.

5. Place the bag bottom piece right side up on the work surface. Position the two pocket flaps on top of this, also right side up. You should have a 1.5cm (½in) gap in-between the two pocket flaps, and the raw edges of the pocket flaps should meet the top raw edge of the bag bottom. Tack (baste) the pocket flaps into position, as shown.

6. Place the bag top piece on top of the bag bottom piece, right sides together, so that the straight edges meet. Sew the bag top and bag bottom pieces together, capturing the pocket flaps in the stitching. Press the seams towards the bag top, interface with the remaining main bag fleece piece and then topstitch the seam at the bag top with a double row of stitches.

7. Place the two blue floral front pocket pieces on top of each other, right sides together. Sew them together along one 40.5cm (16in) edge. Turn the pocket piece

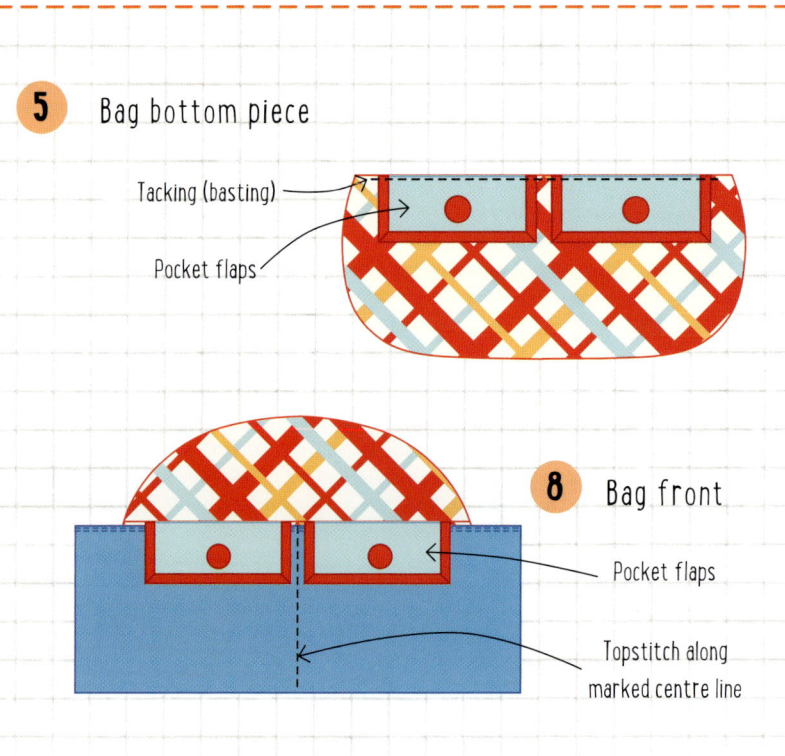

5 Bag bottom piece
- Tacking (basting)
- Pocket flaps

8 Bag front
- Pocket flaps
- Topstitch along marked centre line

SUGAR SWEET SHOULDER BAG

right side out, press, then topstitch the sewn edge with a double row of stitches. Mark a line down the centre of the pocket panel, from the topstitched edge down to the bottom raw edge. Now mark a line approximately 2–2.25cm (¾–⅞in) away from the centre line on each side.

8. Place the pocket panel on top of the bag front, both right sides up. Position the pocket panel so that it is approximately 3mm (⅛in) below the bag top seam (under the pocket flaps) and the marked centre line is centred between the two pocket flaps. Topstitch the pocket panel in place along the centre marked line, as shown.

9. Fold the pocket flaps up out of the way and then fold the front pocket panel, right sides out, along one of the previously marked lines. Press and then topstitch this fold close to the folded edge. Repeat with the remaining marked line. Now fold the two topstitched folds in to meet at the centre stitched line. Machine tack the bottom edge of the pockets into place, as shown. Secure them in place by sewing the bottom 2.5cm (1in) into place over the previous fold topstitching.

10. Mark where the female ends of the magnetic closures should be placed, then insert them into the front side of the pocket panel (see Inserting Magnetic Closures). Trim the pocket panel to match the edges of the bag front and tack all loose edges together.

11. Place one of the piping lengths, right sides together, around the entire edge of the bag front. The raw edge of the piping should lie against the raw edge of the bag front and the piping ends should taper away where they meet at the centre bottom, as shown. Machine tack the piping into place and trim the ends. Repeat with the bag back piece.

12. Centre the zip on top of one of the 39.5 x 6.5cm (15½ x 2½in) check fabric lengths, right sides together, so that one long edge meets. Sew together using the zipper foot. Open the seam, right side out, and press, then topstitch the seam. Repeat with the remaining 39.5 x 6.5cm (15½ x 2½in) strip on the other side of the zip, ensuring that they are aligned. Shorten the zip to meet the ends of the fabric (see Shortening Zips).

13. Place the two ring holder pieces on top of each other, right sides together. Sew together along both of the 15cm (6in) edges, then turn and press. Topstitch along both sewn edges then cut into two 7.5cm (3in) lengths.

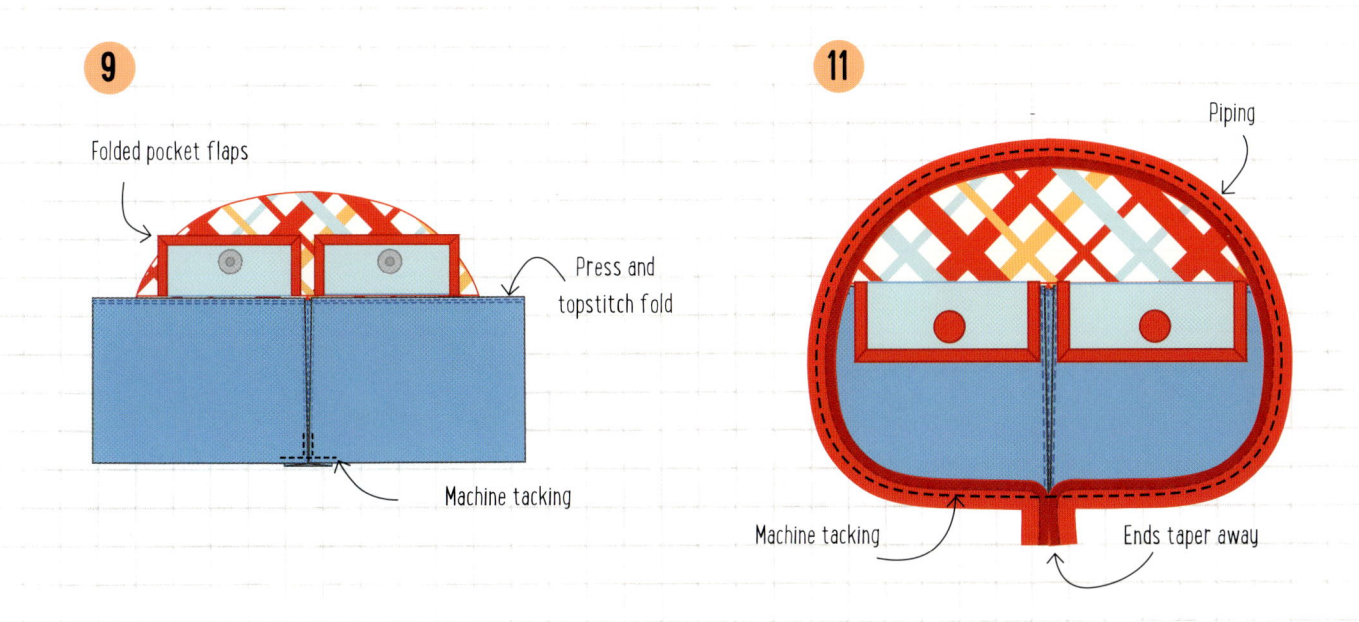

14. Thread one of the 7.5cm (3in) ring holder pieces through one of the oblong handle rings. Fold the fabric onto itself, enclosing the ring then tack the raw edges together. Place the ring and holder on top of one end of the zip panel, right sides together and tack in place, as shown. Repeat this step with the remaining ring and tack to the other side of the zip panel.

15. Place the zip panel and the remaining 54.5 x 12.5cm (21½ x 5in) check fabric panel on top of each other, right sides together. Sew together along both 12.5cm (5in) edges to create a gusset ring – this stitching will also secure the ring holders in position. Topstitch this seam.

Be very careful not to break your needle on the teeth of the zip!

16. Take the bag front and ease one raw side of the gusset ring into place, right sides together, all along the bag front edges. Ensure that the centre top of the bag front is meeting the centre of the zip. Once you are happy with the fit, tack and then sew the gusset neatly and evenly in place. Go over the stitching twice if you need to get closer to the piping. Ensuring first that the zip is partly open for turning, repeat this with the bag back and the remaining edge of the gusset.

17. Take one of the 39.5 x 6.5cm (15½ x 2½in) blue gingham fabric strips and fold under one long edge by approximately 1.5cm (½in). Press well. Repeat with the remaining strip of the same size.

18. Place the 54.5 x 12.5cm (21½ x 5in) gingham fabric strip right sides together with the two folded under strips created in Step 17. There will be approximately a 2cm (¾in) gap in-between the two thinner strips. Sew the ends together to create a gusset ring without the zip, as shown. Topstitch the seams to the 12.5cm (5in) wide panel side.

19. Sew the lining gusset into place with the lining front and back, as you did for the main bag in Step 16. Keeping the main bag right side out and the lining bag right side in, place the lining bag inside the main bag. Neatly and evenly pin the folded under edge of the lining opening around the zip. Ladder stitch the lining in place all the way around the zip (see Useful Stitches).

20. Place the strap and strap lining strips on top of each other, right sides together. Sew together along all four edges, leaving a 5–7.5cm (2–3in) gap in one long edge for turning. Snip the corners and turn right side out (see Turning Handles). Press well then topstitch the strap along all four edges.

21. Insert one end of the strap strips into an oblong ring at one side of the bag. Fold the end under to enclose the rings by approximately 2.5cm (1in), then topstitch the end in place. Repeat on the other side.

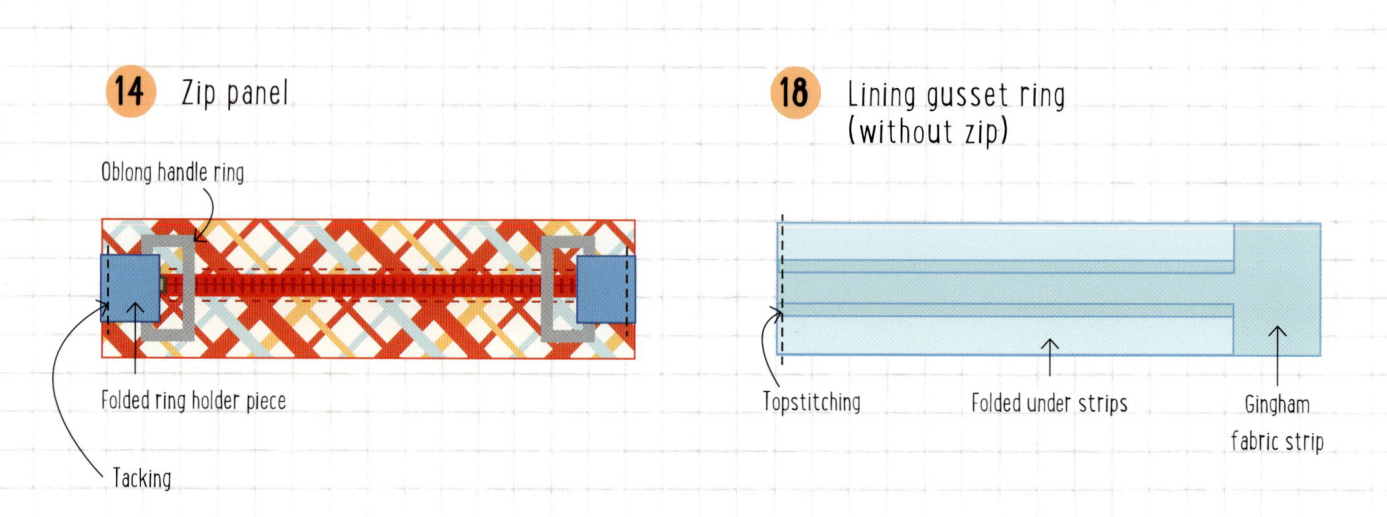

14 Zip panel

Oblong handle ring
Folded ring holder piece
Tacking

18 Lining gusset ring (without zip)

Topstitching
Folded under strips
Gingham fabric strip

80

SUGAR SWEET SHOULDER BAG

WINE & DINE DUO

This fun and frivolous bottle bag and lunch bag make the perfect pair to brighten up your next picnic! The colourful wine bag allows you to bring your own in style on that next dinner date, or it would make the perfect wrapping when giving a fine bottle of wine to a dear friend. The vibrant lunch bag can be used for so many purposes, whether food related or not! It is great as a school lunch bag, as the funky colours and patterns will stand out from the crowd.

SKILL RATING:

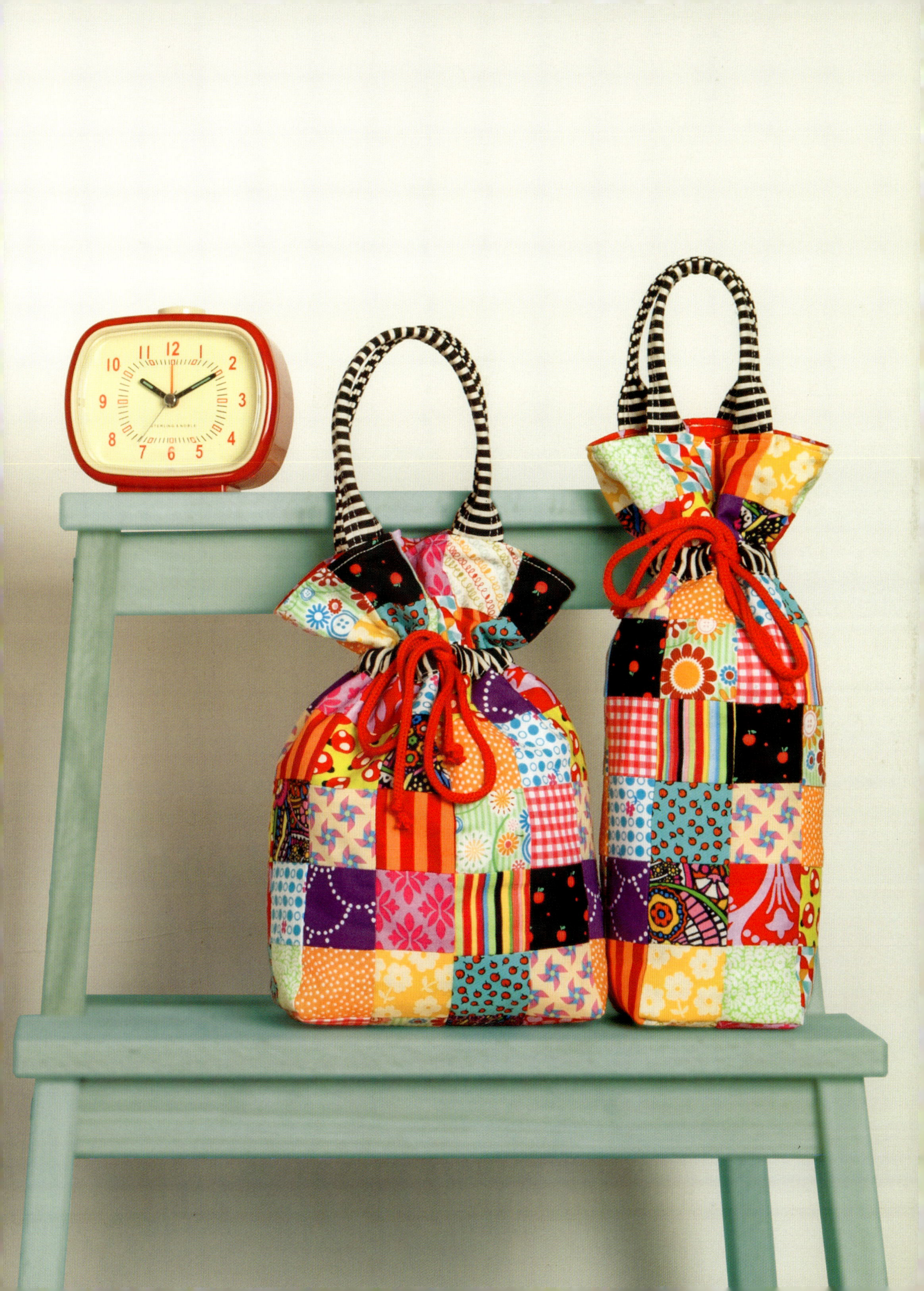

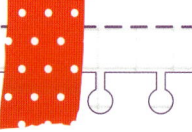

You will need

- A total of 16 strips, each measuring 58.5 x 5cm (23 x 2in), from up to 16 scrap fabrics for main bags
- 15cm (6in) black and white stripe fabric for handles and casings
- 38cm (15in) pink lining fabric
- 43cm (17in) lightweight fusible fleece
- 2m (2¼yd) red cord

Finished sizes: Wine Bag: 35.5 x 10cm (14 x 4in) including handles
Lunch Bag: 32.5 x 16.5cm (13 x 6½in) including handles

WINE & DINE DUO

Cutting

1. Trace all of the Wine and Dine Duo templates (see Pattern Pullout Sheet) onto tracing paper or template plastic, transferring all the markings and cutting them out around the traced lines.

2. From each of the 16 fabric strips, cut one strip measuring 53.5 x 5cm (21 x 2in).

3. From the black and white stripe fabric, cut two strips measuring 4cm (1½in) x the full width of the fabric, one strip measuring 29 x 5.5cm (11½ x 2¼in) for the wine bag casing and one strip measuring 44 x 5.5cm (17¼ x 2¼in) for the lunch bag casing.

4. From the pink lining fabric, trace the wine bag lining and the lunch bag lining templates once and cut out along the traced lines.

5. From the lightweight fusible fleece, trace the wine bag lining and the lunch bag lining templates once (following the interfacing lines) and cut out along the traced lines. Cut two strips measuring 4cm (1½in) x the full width of the fleece.

Preparation

1. Interface one of the handle strips with the matching lightweight fusible fleece strip.

TRY THIS!
Scraps are absolutely perfect for this project! A great way to use those favourite fabric leftovers to whip up fun and festive wine or lunch bags.

Construction

5mm (¼in) seam allowance included.

1. Take eight of the 53.5 x 5cm (21 x 2in) fabric strips and sew them randomly together along the 53.5cm (21in) edges. Press well, then repeat with the remaining eight fabric strips until you have two pieced panels, each measuring 32 x 53.5cm (12½ x 21in), as shown.

2. Place the panels from Step 1 on your cutting mat. Neaten one 32cm (12½in) edge, then cut across the piecing to create ten pieced strips, each measuring 32 x 5cm (12½ x 2in). Repeat with the remaining panel so you now have twenty pieced strips, each consisting of eight squares, as shown.

WINE BAG

3. Take eight of the pieced strips created in Step 2 and sew together along the 32cm (12½in) edges to create a chequerboard panel, as shown.

When creating the chequerboard panel, alternate the different strips and flip every second strip so that no two identical fabrics will meet.

4. From the remaining scraps of the 5cm (2in) wide strips, cut four 5cm (2in) squares. Sew two squares together along one edge and press. Repeat to make two strips of two squares and then sew these on to the bottom edge of the main wine bag panel, as shown. Press, then interface the panel with the matching piece of fusible fleece. The fleece will be 5mm (¼in) narrower along both side edges.

5. Take the strip of striped wine bag casing and fold it in half, right sides together, along the length. Sew together along both short ends and one long edge, leaving a 2.5cm (1in) gap in the centre for turning. Snip the corners and turn right side out (see Turning Handles), then press well.

6. Position the casing onto the wine bag panel, as shown. The casing should sit centred within the width, over the seam of the 2nd and 3rd row of chequerboard. Topstitch in place very near to the edge, along both 27.5m (11in) edges only (see Useful Stitches).

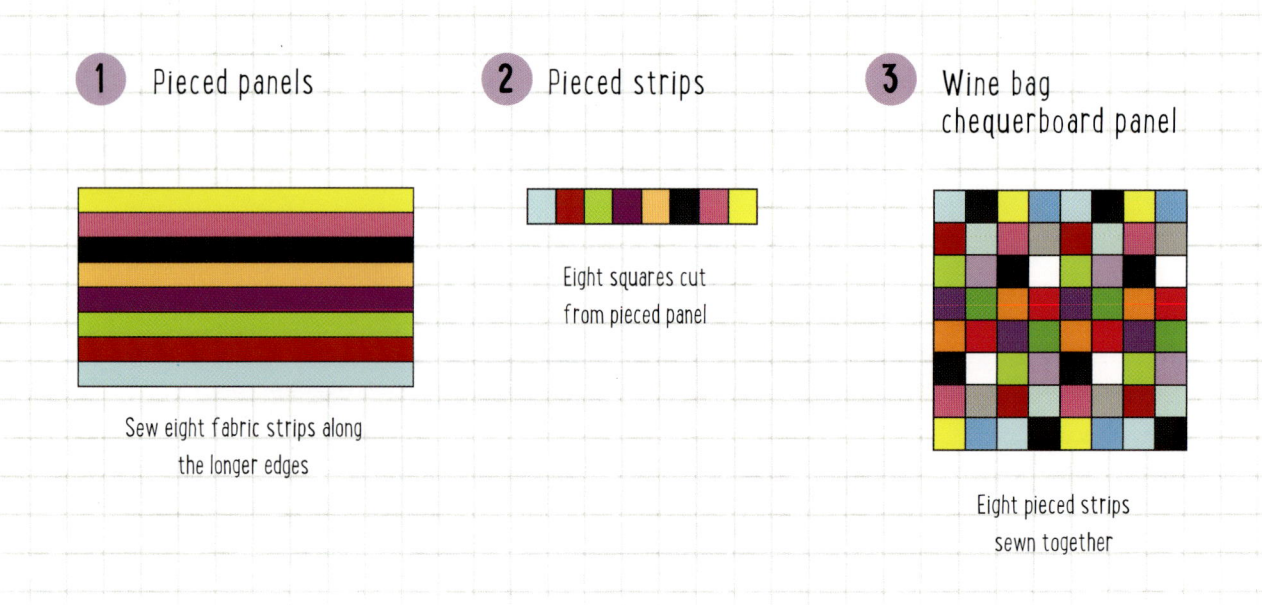

1 Pieced panels

Sew eight fabric strips along the longer edges

2 Pieced strips

Eight squares cut from pieced panel

3 Wine bag chequerboard panel

Eight pieced strips sewn together

WINE & DINE DUO

7. Fold the wine bag panel in half, right sides together, so that the two side edges meet. Sew together along the side edge and bottom edge along the two squares, leaving the raw angled bottom corner unsewn for now.

8. Sew the box corners into place at both bottom corners of your wine bag (see Cut Out Box Corners).

9. Repeat Steps 7 and 8 with the wine bag lining piece, leaving a 12.5cm (5in) gap in the middle of the side edge for turning.

10. Place the two handle strips on top of each other, right sides together. Sew them together along both long edges and one short end, leaving one short end open for turning. Turn (see Turning Handles), cut off the sewn end and press the handle strip well. Topstitch the handle strip along both long edges with a double row of stitching. Cut two 20cm (8in) lengths for the handles and put the rest aside.

11. Fold one of the handle lengths onto itself along the length. Topstitch the handle in this folded position, starting and ending 2.5cm (1in) from each end. Repeat with the second handle.

12. Turn the main wine bag right side out. Position the handle onto the bag front (where the casing opening is), right sides together, matching the handle sides up with the outer edge of the centre two squares, as shown. Tack (baste) in place (see Useful Stitches). Repeat with the remaining handle on the bag back.

13. Keeping the main bag right side out and the lining bag right side in, place the main bag inside the lining bag. Carefully sew all the way around the top of the bag, capturing the handle ends in your sewing. Turn the bag right side out through the gap in the lining and push the lining inside the main bag. Press, then topstitch the opening all the way around the top edges of the bag. Ladder stitch the opening in the lining closed (see Useful Stitches).

14. Take a 86.5cm (34in) length of red cord and secure a safety pin to one end. Using the safety pin to guide it through, insert and pull the cord all the way through the casing. Tie it in a bow and when you decide on the length you want, tie the ends and trim.

Place sticky tape around the ends of the cord before cutting to avoid fraying during use.

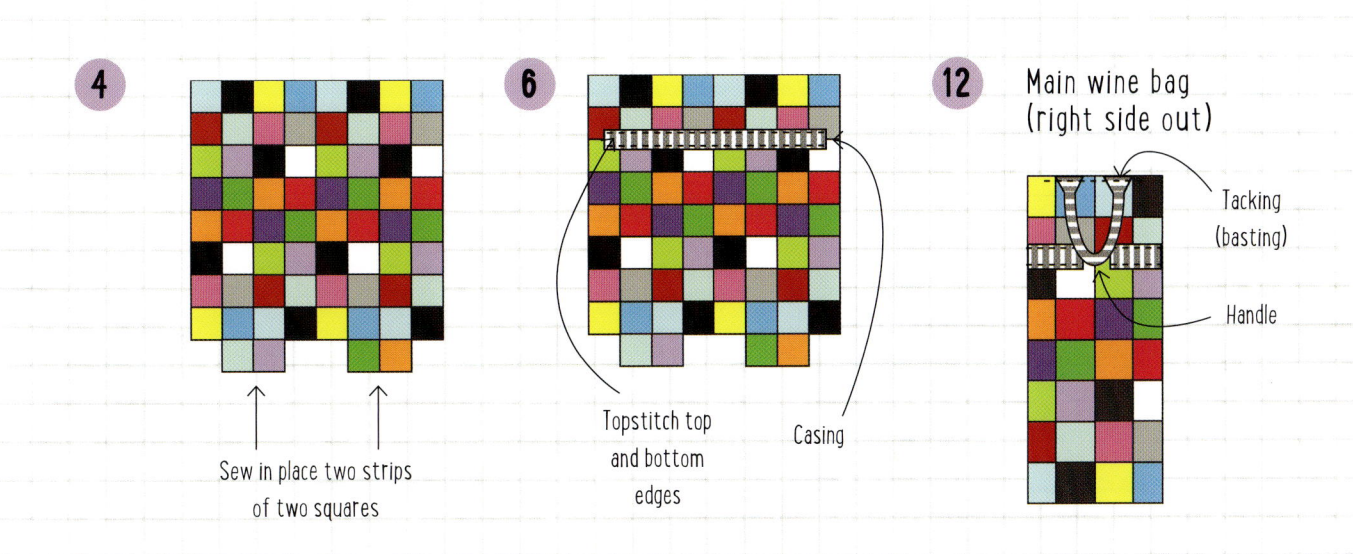

4 Sew in place two strips of two squares

6 Topstitch top and bottom edges — Casing

12 Main wine bag (right side out) — Tacking (basting) — Handle

LUNCH BAG

15. Take the remaining twelve pieced strips. Shorten four strips (two of each type) by removing one end square, so they are now seven squares long. Alternating the different strips and flipping every second same strip so that no two identical fabrics will meet, sew the twelve strips together to create a chequerboard panel, as shown. Interface the panel with the matching piece of fusible fleece – the fleece will be 5mm (¼in) narrower along both side edges.

16. Fold the strip of lunch bag casing in half, right sides together, all the way along the length. Sew together along both short ends and one long edge, leaving a 2.5cm (1in) gap in the centre of your sewing for turning. Snip the corners and turn right side out (see Turning Handles), then press well.

17. Position the casing onto the lunch bag panel, as you did with the wine bag in Step 6. The casing should sit centred within the width, over the seam of the second and third row of the chequerboard.

Topstitch in place very close to the edge along the 43cm (17in) edges only. Now fold the panel in half, right sides together, so that the two side edges meet, and sew in place. Open and refold the bag so the four squares at the bottom back and bottom front meet evenly. Sew the bottom raw edges of the four squares together, leaving the raw angled edge at each bottom corner unsewn for now.

18. Sew the box corners into place at both bottom corners of your lunch bag (see Cut Out Box Corners).

19. Repeat Steps 17–18 (omitting casing steps) with the lunch bag lining piece, leaving a 12.5cm (5in) gap in the middle of the side edge for turning.

20. Cut the remaining handle strip into two 25cm (10in) lengths. Take one of the handle pieces and fold it onto itself along the length. Topstitch the handle in this folded position, starting and ending 2.5cm (1in) from each end. Repeat with the second handle.

21. Turn the main lunch bag right side out. Position the handle onto the bag front (where the casing opening is), right sides together, matching the handle sides up outside the centre two squares, as shown. Tack (baste) in place. Repeat with the remaining handle on the bag back.

22. Keeping the main bag right side out and the lining right side in, place the main bag inside the lining bag. Carefully sew all the way around the top of the bag, capturing the bag handle ends in your sewing. Turn the bag right side out through the gap in the lining and push the lining inside the main bag. Press and then topstitch the opening all the way around the top edges of the bag. Ladder stitch the opening in the lining closed (see Useful Stitches).

23. Take a 96.5cm (38in) length of red cord and secure a safety pin to one end. Using the safety pin to guide it through, insert and pull the cord all the way through the casing. Tie in a bow and when you decide on the length you want, tie the ends and trim.

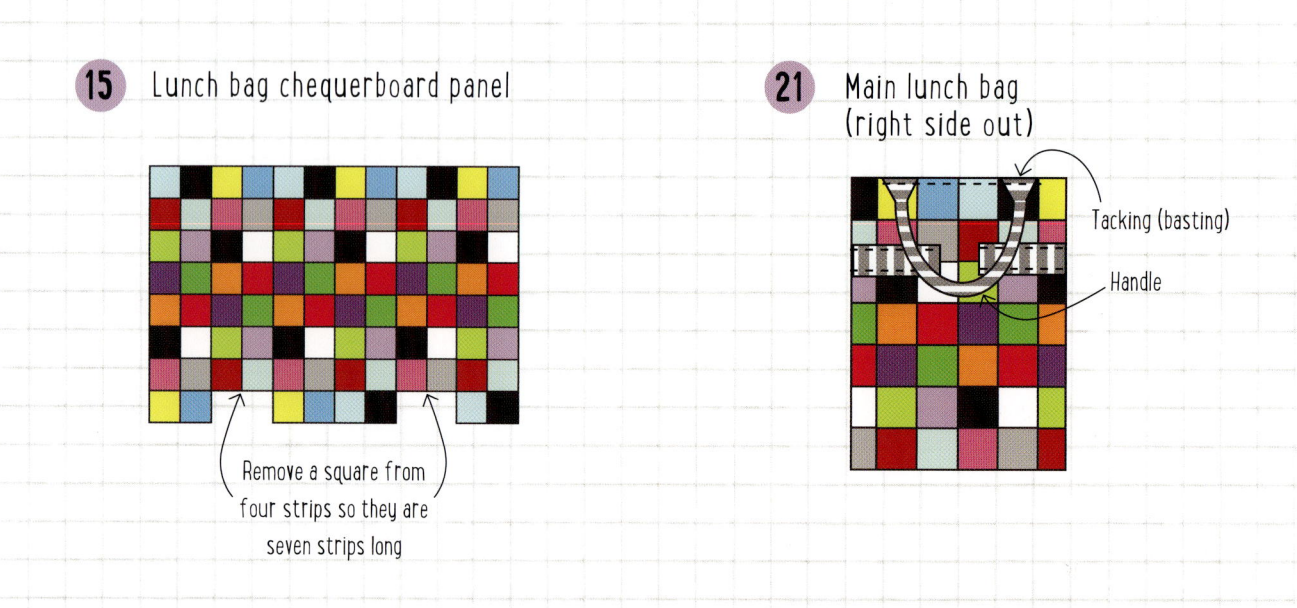

15 Lunch bag chequerboard panel

Remove a square from four strips so they are seven strips long

21 Main lunch bag (right side out)

Tacking (basting)

Handle

WINE & DINE DUO

LUSCIOUS LAYERED BAG

I designed this sweet layered shoulder bag with young girls or 'tweens' in mind, and it just makes me wish that I were a little girl all over again! I know that my own daughter is wishing for one this Christmas. The layers can be made up with fabrics in any colours, patterns and textures to match the latest trends – a must for fashion-conscious tweens!. Just imagine this cute bag teamed up with a matching outfit using fabrics from your little girl's favourite collection – simply adorable!

SKILL RATING:

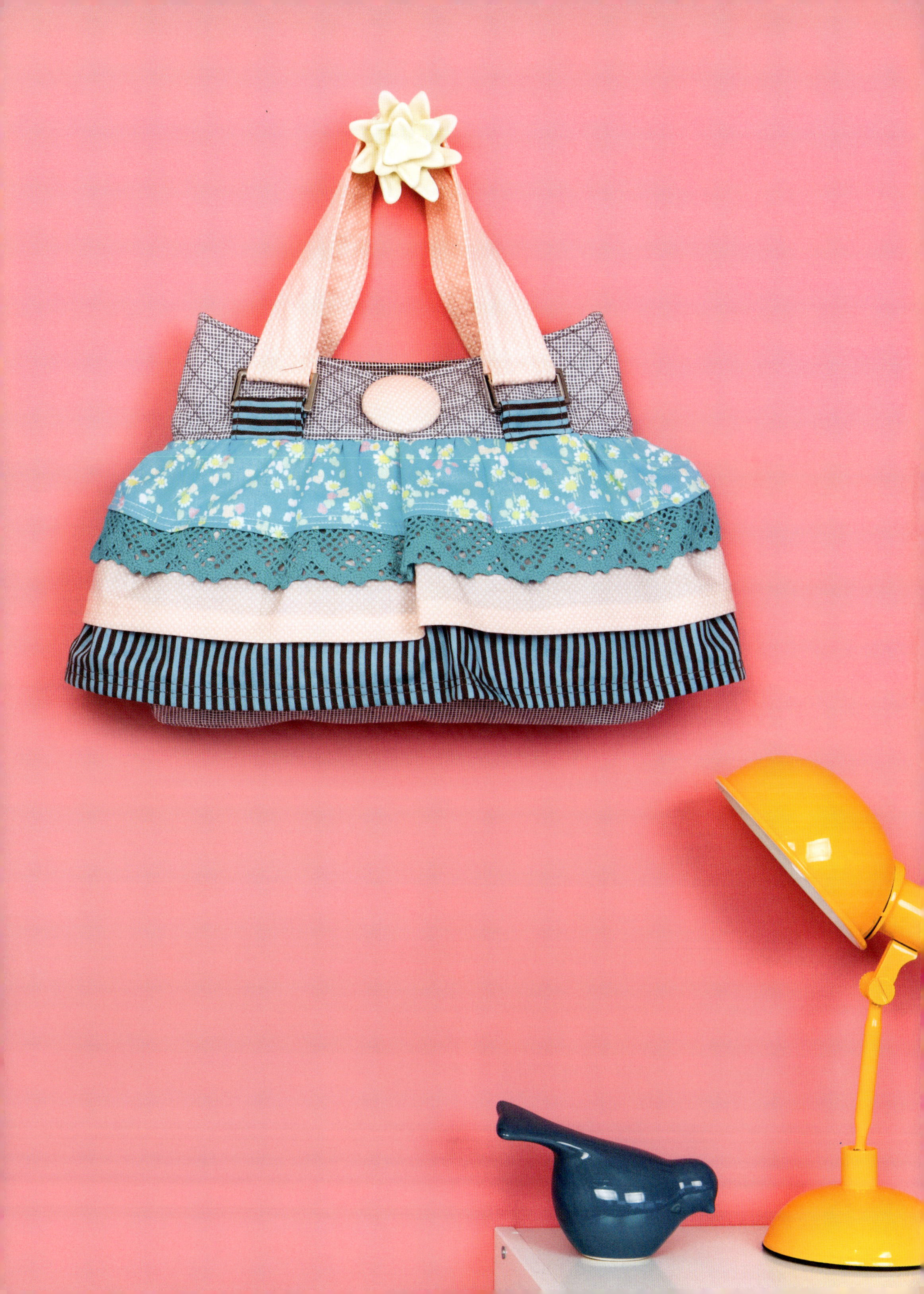

You will need

- 40cm (15¾in) grey basic print fabric for bag top, bottom and lining
- 10cm (4in) aqua floral print fabric for top ruffle
- 25cm (10in) pink spot print fabric for second ruffle and handles
- 18cm (7in) aqua and grey stripe print fabric for third ruffle and ring loop
- 30cm (12in) lightweight fusible fleece
- 85cm (33in) aqua lace or other matching trim
- Four 4cm (1½in) oblong rings
- 4cm (1½in) self-covering button or similar
- Erasable marking pencil

Finished size: 32 x 34cm (12½ x 13½in) including handles

LUSCIOUS LAYERED BAG

Cutting

1. Trace the Luscious Layered Bag templates (see Pattern Pullout Sheet) onto tracing paper or template plastic, transferring all the markings and cutting them out around the traced lines.

2. From the grey basic print fabric, trace the main bag top template twice, the main bag bottom template twice and the lining templates twice onto the fabric, and cut out along the traced lines.

3. From the aqua floral print fabric, cut one strip measuring 9 x 81cm (3½ x 32in).

4. From the pink spot print fabric, cut one strip measuring 14 x 81cm (5½ x 32in) and four strips measuring 5 x 40cm (2 x 16in) for the handles.

5. From the aqua and grey print fabric, cut one strip measuring 16.5 x 81cm (6½ x 32in) and eight strips each measuring 7.5 x 5cm (3 x 2in) for the ring closures.

6. From the lightweight fusible fleece, trace the main bag top template twice and the main bag bottom template twice onto the fleece, and cut out along the traced lines. Now cut two strips measuring 5 x 40cm (2 x 15¾in) for the handles.

Preparation

1. Cover the self-covering button with remaining pink spot print fabric, interfaced with fleece, following the manufacturer's instructions.

2. Take the two main bag top pieces, two main bag bottom pieces and two of the handle strips and interface these with the fusible fleece pieces of the same size.

3. Mark a 1.5cm (½in) diagonal grid onto the bag top pieces using an erasable marking pencil. Using a dark grey thread, machine quilt these lines into place on the bag top pieces.

93

Construction

5mm (¼in) seam allowance included.

1. Place the two bag top pieces on top of each other, right sides together. Sew together along the two side edges only.

2. Place the two main bag bottom pieces on top of each other with right sides together. Sew together along the side and bottom edges only. Follow the box corners technique (see Box Corners), sewing across where the triangle measures 4cm (1½in), and turn right sides out.

3. Take the aqua floral ruffle strip, fold under one long 81cm (32in) edge by approximately 1cm (⅜in) and press in place. Fold the folded edge under again by approximately 1.5cm (½in) to create a neat hem edge and press well again.

4. Lay the aqua floral ruffle strip right side up on your work surface. Position the length of aqua lace under and along the bottom folded hem edge of the ruffle strip so that they overlap by approximately 5mm (¼in). Pin in place then topstitch the hem 3mm (⅛in) and 5mm (¼in) from the folded edge (see Useful Stitches), capturing the lace in position at the same time. Trim the excess ends of the lace.

5. Repeat Step 3 with the pink spot ruffle strip. Pin in place and then topstitch the hem 3mm (⅛in) and 5mm (¼in) from the folded edge.

6. Lay the aqua and grey ruffle strip right side up on your work surface. Position the pink ruffle strip right side up on top of this, so that the top raw 81cm (32in) edges meet. Now place the aqua lace trimmed strip on top of this in the same way, as shown. Sew the three layers together, close to the top raw edge.

7. Fold the ruffle sandwich in half, right sides together, from one side edge to the other so that all of the raw ruffle edges meet neatly. Pin and sew together along this side raw edge. Press the seam open and then turn right side out.

8. Hem the bottom edge of the striped ruffle layer by folding under by approximately 1cm (⅜in) and pressing in place. Fold this folded edge under again by

6 Three ruffle layers

Raw top edges meet · Sew to secure together

LUSCIOUS LAYERED BAG

approximately 1.5cm (½in) to create a neat hem edge and press well again. Pin in place and then topstitch the hem 3mm (⅛in) and 5mm (¼in) from the folded edge.

To avoid fraying of the top edge when gathering, first neaten the raw edge with a zigzag or overlocking stitch.

9. Hand sew small-to-medium running stitches all the way around the top raw edge of the ruffle loop. Pull and gather the running stitches evenly along the edge until the diameter of the top ruffle edge measures the same as the diameter of the bag bottom opening. Secure well with a knot.

10. Take the bag bottom, right sides out, and fit the ruffles on top so that the top gathered edge of the ruffle loop meets the top raw edge of the bag bottom. The seam in the ruffle loop should be positioned at the centre back of the bag bottom. Machine tack (baste) the top raw edges in place (see Useful Stitches).

11. Place two of the aqua and grey stripe ring closure strips on top of each other, right sides together, and sew together along both 7.5cm (3in) edges. Turn and press then topstitch the two 7.5cm (3in) sewn edges. Thread the ring closure strip through an oblong ring and fold onto itself to create a loop, enclosing the ring, as shown in the photograph. Tack the ends in place to secure. Repeat to create three more ring loops.

12. Take the bag bottom (with ruffles) and position two of the ring loops, right sides together, onto the bag front, over the ruffles, so that the raw edge of the loop meets the raw edge of the ruffles. The loops should be approximately 4cm (1½in) in from the bag sides, as shown. Machine tack in place. Repeat on the bag back.

12 Bag front

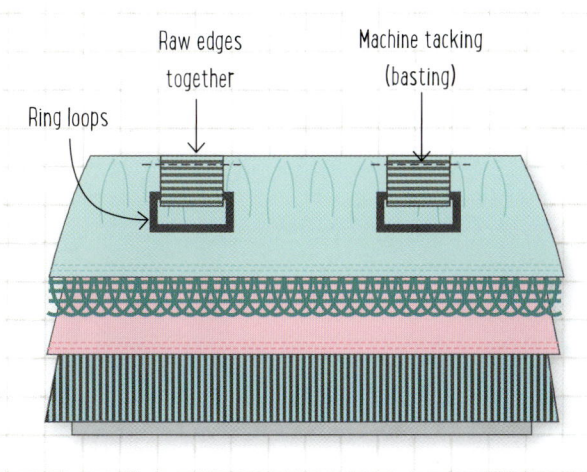

Ring loops — Raw edges together — Machine tacking (basting)

13. Take the bag top and, keeping it inside out, fit it top side first over the bag bottom layers. The bottom raw edge of the bag top should now be right sides together with the top raw edge of the bag bottom. The ruffles and ring loops will lie sandwiched in-between. Pin securely in place, then sew all of the layers together all the way around the bag, taking care due to the thickness of the fabric.

14. Turn the bag top right side out so that it forms the top of the bag. Position the ring loops facing upwards and press in place. Topstitch the bag top 3mm (⅛in) from the seam, capturing the ring loops in the sewing to keep them facing upwards.

15. Place the two bag lining pieces on top of each other with right sides together. Sew the lining pieces together along the side and bottom edges only, leaving a 12.5cm (5in) gap along the centre of the bottom edge for turning. Follow the box corners technique (see Box Corners), sewing across where the triangle measures 4cm (1½in).

16. Keeping the main bag right side out and the lining bag right side in, place the main bag inside the lining bag. Pin carefully and evenly and then sew all the way around the top of the bag opening. Turn the bag right side out through the gap in the bottom of the lining and push the lining inside the main bag. Press and then topstitch all the way around the top bag edge.

17. Take one handle strip with fleece and one without fleece and place these on top of each other, right sides together. Sew together along all four edges, leaving a 5cm (2in) gap in one long edge for turning. Snip the corners, turn right side out (see Turning Handles) and press well. Sew along all four edges of the handle with a double row of topstitching. Take the ends of the handle and insert these into both of the oblong rings at the front of the bag. Fold the ends under to enclose the rings by approximately 2cm (¾in) and topstitch the ends in place. Repeat to make the handle for the back of the bag.

18. Sew the covered button into the desired position at the centre top of the bag front, accessing this through the gap in the lining. The button is purely for decorative purposes. Finally, ladder stitch the turning gap closed (see Useful Stitches).

If you have difficulty finding oblong handle rings, do not worry. Any rings will work for the bag, as long as they are at least 4cm (1½in) in diameter.

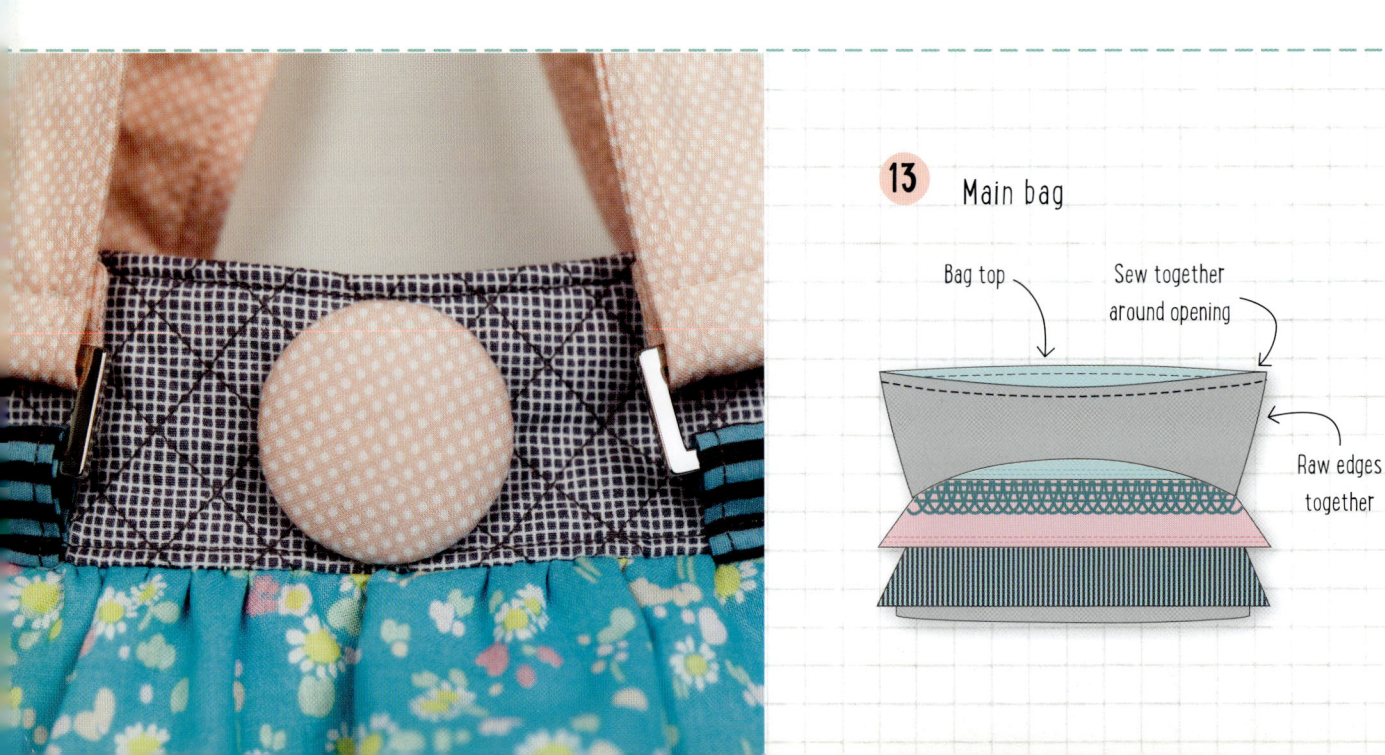

13 Main bag

Bag top — Sew together around opening

Raw edges together

LUSCIOUS LAYERED BAG

RUFFLE DUFFLE

Ruffle Duffle is the perfect overnight or sports bag; highly practical while at the same time being completely cute and girlie. It would make an ideal gift for any special women in your life, from the sporty teen to the jet-setting businesswoman. Or why not make one for a boy? Simply leave out the ruffle and choose some of his favourite masculine prints.

SKILL RATING:

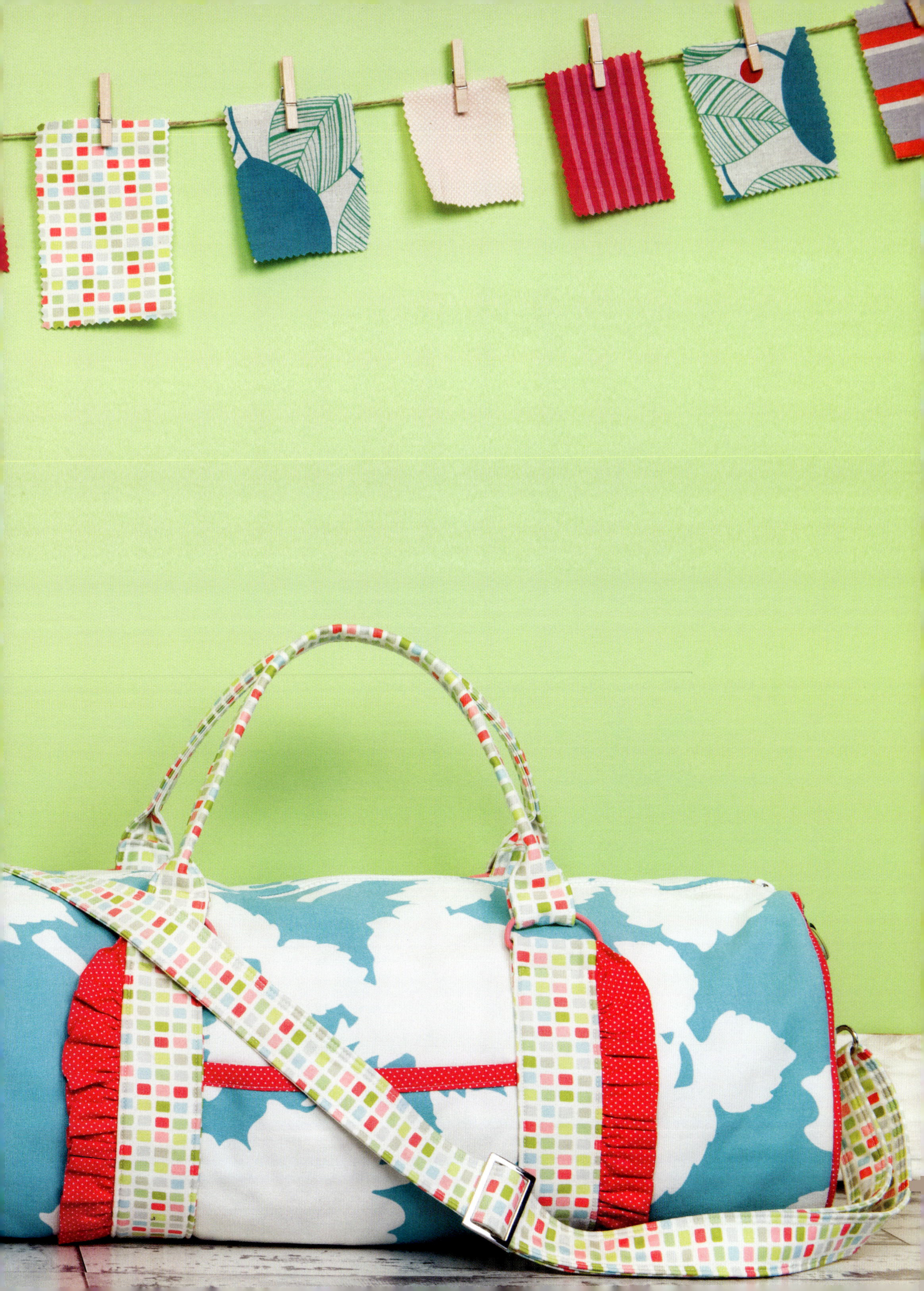

You will need

- 90cm (35½in) blue home décor weight print fabric for main bag
- 61cm (24in) lining fabric
- 90cm (35½in) multi-square home décor weight print fabric for handles and end pockets
- 22.5cm (9in) pink micro-spot print fabric for ruffle and binding
- An extra fat quarter (18 x 22in) of pink micro-spot print fabric to make piping and bias tape or 2m (2¼yd) of pre-made bias tape
- 1m (40in) lightweight fusible fleece
- 2m (2¼yd) white cord to make piping
- Two matching 2.5cm (1in) buttons
- 61cm (24in) white chunky open-end zip
- Four large 5cm (2in) and two medium 3.3cm (1¼in) D-Rings
- Three large 4cm (1½in) swivel hooks
- Large 4cm (1½in) slide adjuster
- Decorative zip pull (optional)

Finished size: 54 x 25cm (21½ x 10in) excluding handles

RUFFLE DUFFLE

Cutting

1. Trace all of the Ruffle Duffle templates (see Pattern Pullout Sheet) onto tracing paper or template plastic, transferring all the markings and cutting them out around the traced lines.

2. From the main blue home décor weight print fabric, cut one large 58.5 x 77.5cm (23 x 30½in) panel for the main outer bag, two 25 x 48cm (10 x 19in) pieces for the centre pockets, and four 4.5 x 9.5cm (1¾ x 3in) pieces for the shoulder strap ring holders. Trace the bag end template twice onto fabric, and cut out along the traced lines.

3. From the lining fabric, cut one large 58.5 x 77.5cm (23 x 30½in) panel for the main lining bag. Trace the bag end template twice onto fabric and cut out along the traced lines.

4. From the multi-square home décor weight print fabric, trace the end pocket template four times and cut out along the traced lines. Cut four 70 x 6.5cm (27½ x 2½in) strips for the ring holder strips, four 58.5 x 5cm (23 x 2in) strips for the main handles and four 76 x 5cm (30 x 2in) strips for the long adjustable shoulder strap.

5. From the pink micro-spot print fabric, cut two strips measuring 7.5cm (3in) x the full fabric width for the ruffles and four strips measuring 5 x 25cm (2 x 10in) for the pocket bindings.

6. From the lightweight fusible fleece, cut one large panel measuring 58.5 x 77.5cm (23 x 30½in) for the main outer bag. Trace the bag end template twice and cut out along the traced lines. Now cut two 70 x 6.5cm (27½ x 2½in) strips for the ring holder strips, two 58.5 x 5cm (23 x 2in) strips for the main handles and two 75.5 x 5cm (29¾ x 2in) strips for the long adjustable shoulder straps.

Preparation

1. Interface the main bag panel, half of the handle strips and the main bag end pieces with the matching fusible fleece pieces. The shoulder strap interfacing is slightly shorter on one end than the fabric – this is intentional.

2. Create two 1m (40in) lengths of piping with the pink fabric bias strips and white cord (see Creating Piping). From the remainder of the fat quarter of pink micro-spot fabric make two 91.5cm (36in) lengths of 2.5cm (1in) bias tape.

Construction

5mm (¼in) seam allowance included.

1. Take the interfaced main bag panel, lining panel and chunky zip. Undo and separate the two sides of the zip. Create a sandwich of three layers by placing the main bag panel right side up, then one side of the zip centered right side down on top of one 58.5cm (23in) edge, and finally the lining panel right side down so that all the raw edges meet. Pin or tack (baste) evenly in place (see Useful Stitches). Using the zipper foot on your machine, sew the zip in place along the 58.5cm (23in) edge.

2. Repeat to make the three layers, this time with the remaining zip side on the opposite 58.5cm (23in) edge of the main bag and lining panel. Ensure that the zip ends are facing in the same direction and the zip is equally centred so the two sides will join evenly later. Sew in place with the zipper foot. Turn the main bag and lining layers right side out. Neatly press the zip seams and then topstitch the bag panel along both zip seams (see Useful Stitches).

3. Take the two centre side pocket pieces measuring 25 x 48cm (10 x 19in) and place them on top of each other, right sides out. Machine tack them together along all four edges.

> Any zip may be used for this project, as long as it is an open-end zip. If you want to make construction and zip sewing easier choose a lighter-weight plastic zip.

4. Fold one of the 5 x 25cm (2 x 10in) pink binding strips in half along the length, right side out, and press. Now fold the long raw edges into the fold and press again. Use this strip to bind one 25cm (10in) edge of the pocket panel (see Topstitch Binding). Repeat to bind the other end of the pocket panel and then set aside.

5. Fold one of the 7.5cm (3in) pink spot ruffle strips in half, right sides out, all the way along the length. Press well. Securing the end of a double length of strong thread, sew small/medium running stitches by hand all the way along the raw edge of the folded strip. Pull and gather the running stitches evenly along the edge, until the length of the ruffle strip measures approximately 61cm (24in). Tie off the thread and then machine sew the raw edge to secure the ruffles.

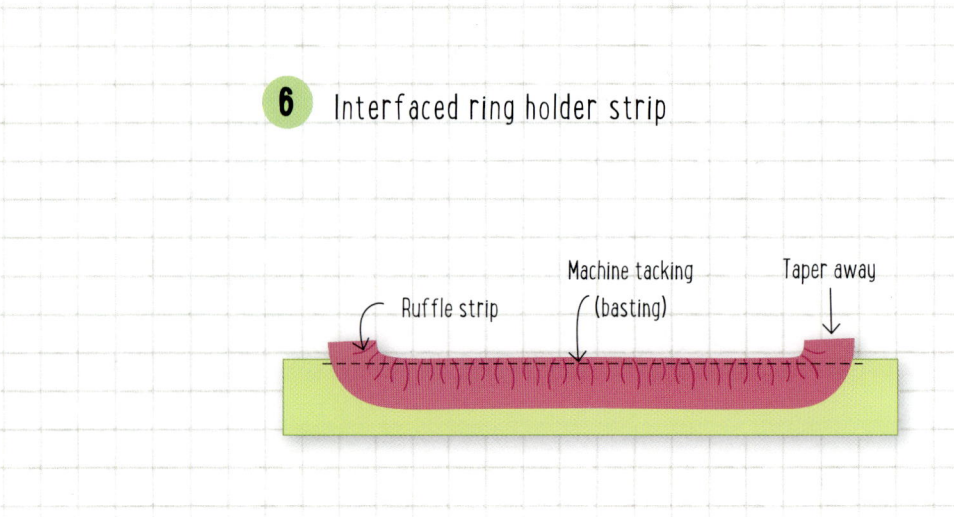

6 Interfaced ring holder strip

- Ruffle strip
- Machine tacking (basting)
- Taper away

RUFFLE DUFFLE

6. Lay one of the 70 x 6.5cm (27½ x 2½in) interfaced ring holder strips right side up on your work surface. Place the ruffle, right sides together, along one side edge of the fabric strip. The raw edge of the ruffle should lie against the raw edge of the fabric and the ruffle should taper away from the strip 5cm (2in) from either end, as shown. Machine tack the ruffle into place and trim the excess ends.

7. Take one of the non-interfaced ring holder strips and place it right sides together with the strip with the ruffle. Pin securely and then sew together along all four edges, leaving a 7.5cm (3in) gap in the centre of the long edge without the ruffle. Snip the corners, turn right side out and press well. Repeat Steps 5–7 to create another ring holder strip.

8. Place the main bag panel right side up on your work surface. Place the bound centre pocket panel right side up on top of the main bag panel, ensuring that it is completely central. Tack (baste) the raw side edges evenly in place and machine sew across the centre of the pocket panel to create two pockets.

9. Now take one of the ruffle ring holder strips. Thread both ends of the strip through a 5cm (2in) D ring, fold the ends under by approximately 2.5cm (1in) and pin in place. Lay the ruffle strip with rings right side up on top of the main bag panel, so that it covers the raw tacked side of the pocket panel. Tack evenly and then topstitch in place along all edges. The short ends of your topstitching need to capture the folded-under ends, enclosing the D-rings. Repeat with the remaining ruffle strip.

10. Place two multi-print end pocket pieces on top of each other, right sides out. Machine tack together along all edges. Repeat with the remaining two end pocket pieces.

11. Fold one of the 25cm (10in) pink binding strips in half along its length, right side out, and press. Now fold the long raw edges into the fold and press again. Use this strip to bind the top straight edge of one of your end pockets (see Topstitch Binding). Repeat to bind the second end pocket.

12. Place two of the 4.5 x 9.5cm (1¾ x 3¾in) shoulder strap ring pieces on top of each other, right sides together. Sew together along all four edges, leaving a 2.5cm (1in) gap along one long edge for turning. Snip the corners, turn and press. Thread this through one of the medium D-rings and pin the ends evenly in place.

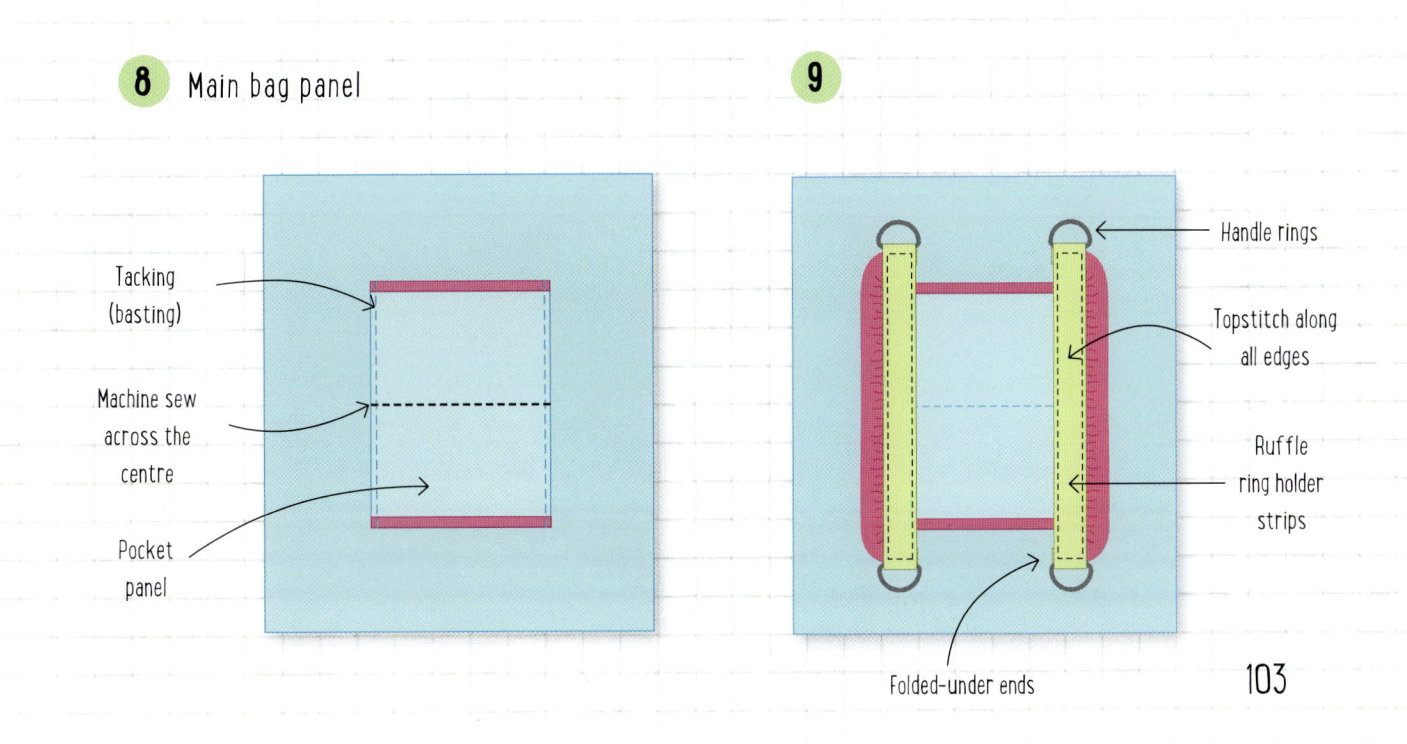

8 Main bag panel
- Tacking (basting)
- Machine sew across the centre
- Pocket panel

9
- Handle rings
- Topstitch along all edges
- Ruffle ring holder strips
- Folded-under ends

13. Place one of the interfaced main bag end pieces and one of the lining bag end pieces evenly on top of each other, right sides out. Position one of the end pockets on top of this so that the curved edges meet. Machine tack the raw pocket edges in place, approximately 3mm (⅛in) from the raw edges. Tack the remaining section of the bag end edges together in the same way.

14. Position the D-ring loop approximately 0.5–1.5cm (⅛–½in) above the centre of the pocket. Machine sew this in place through all of the layers, and then sew a decorative pink button over the stitching.

15. Place one of the lengths of piping with right sides together around the complete edge of one of the bag ends. The raw edge of the piping should lie against the raw edge of the fabric, and the piping ends should taper away from the bag where they meet at the centre bottom, as shown. Machine tack in place and trim the ends. Repeat with the other bag end piece.

When sewing piped sections in place, you will find it easier if you use a zipper foot. This will ensure you set - your stitching as close as possible to the cord in your piping - and give a neater piped end.

16. Take the main bag and connect both sides of the open-end zip. Zip the bag shut and then turn the bag inside out. Take one of the bag ends and ease it into place, right sides together, at the zip joining mechanism end of the main bag. Ensure that the centre top of the bag end meets the zip on the main bag. Tack neatly and evenly into place. Once you are happy with the fit, sew the bag side into place. When you reach the zip section, be very careful not to break your needle, but ensure that the needle takes its stitches between the teeth of the zip. Go over the stitching twice if you need to, and trim away any excess zip.

17. Before moving on to the following step, turn your bag end side right side out and check that the piping is nice and neat. If the stitching needs to get closer to the piping, simply sew around the bag end again, increasing the seam allowance a little.

18. Take the length of bias tape created in Step 2 of Preparation and bind the raw lining seam at the bag end. This will neaten the bag lining and keep the seams strong. To do this, simply fold the bias tape in half, right sides out, and then fit the tape over the seam allowance so that the raw edge of the seam

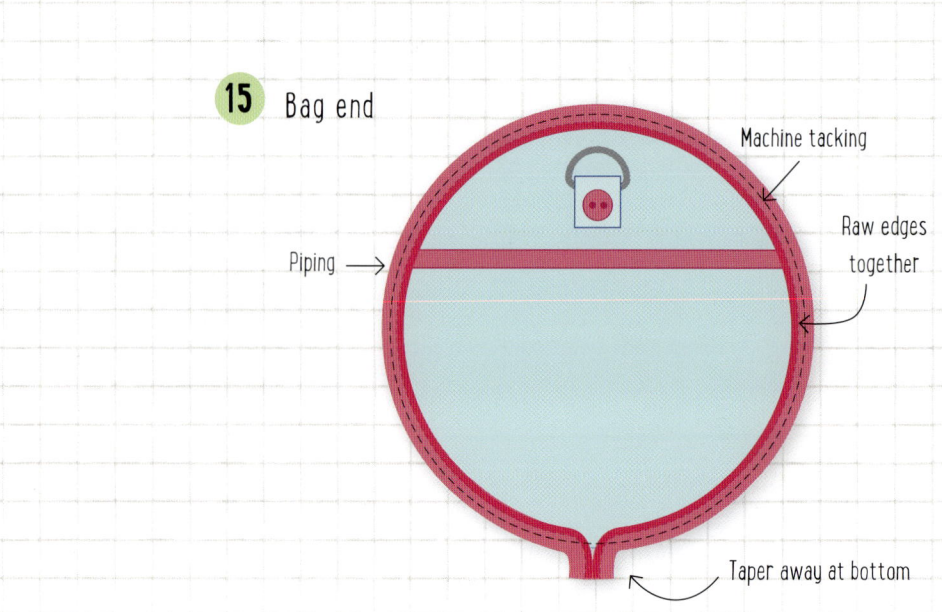

15 Bag end

- Machine tacking
- Piping
- Raw edges together
- Taper away at bottom

RUFFLE DUFFLE

sits inside the bias fold. Pin or tack (baste) securely, then topstitch in place. When you get to the end, simply cut the end of the bias tape, fold it under slightly and continue to topstitch the neat folded end in place, slightly overlapping the starting point.

19. Open the zip halfway and repeat Steps 16–18 with the remaining bag end. This time, make sure you meet both zip sides together evenly when tacking and sewing the top section.

20. Place one interfaced and one non-interfaced handle strip on top of each other, right sides together. Sew together along all four edges, leaving a 5–7.5cm (2–3in) gap in one long edge for turning. Snip the corners, turn right side out (see Turning Handles) and press well. Topstitch the handle along all four edges. Fold the handle onto itself all the way along the length and then topstitch the handle in this folded position, starting and ending 9cm (3½in) from both short ends. Topstitch this together by stitching over the previous topstitching. Insert the ends into both of the D-rings at one side of the bag. Fold the ends under to enclose the rings by approximately 2.5cm (1in) and then topstitch the ends in place. Repeat to create the second handle.

21. Sew the two interfaced shoulder strap pieces together at the short ends where the interfacing did not reach all the way (the 5mm (¼in) seam allowance should have no interfacing). Press the seam open. Sew the two remaining non-interfaced strap pieces together along one short end. Press the seam open.

22. Place the two strap pieces on top of each other, right sides together, and sew together along all four edges, leaving a 7.5–10cm (3–4in) gap along one long edge for turning. Snip the corners, turn and press (see Turning Handles). Topstitch the strap along all edges. Attach one end of the strap to your slide adjuster (see Adjustable Straps), and then attach the two swivel hooks. Now attach the adjustable strap to the D-rings at the bag ends.

Use fabric protector on your duffle bag before use to keep it looking fresh and lovely throughout regular use.

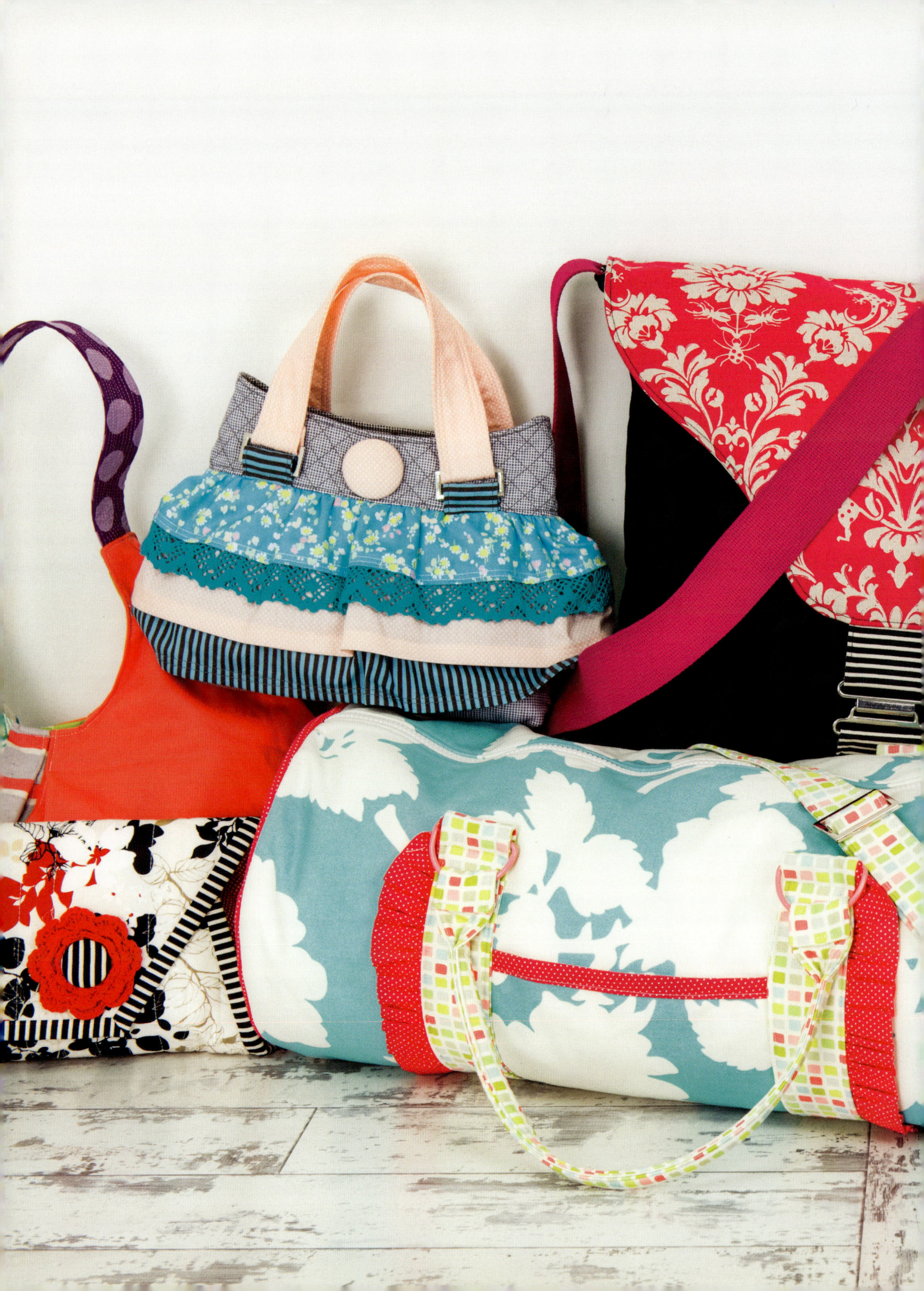

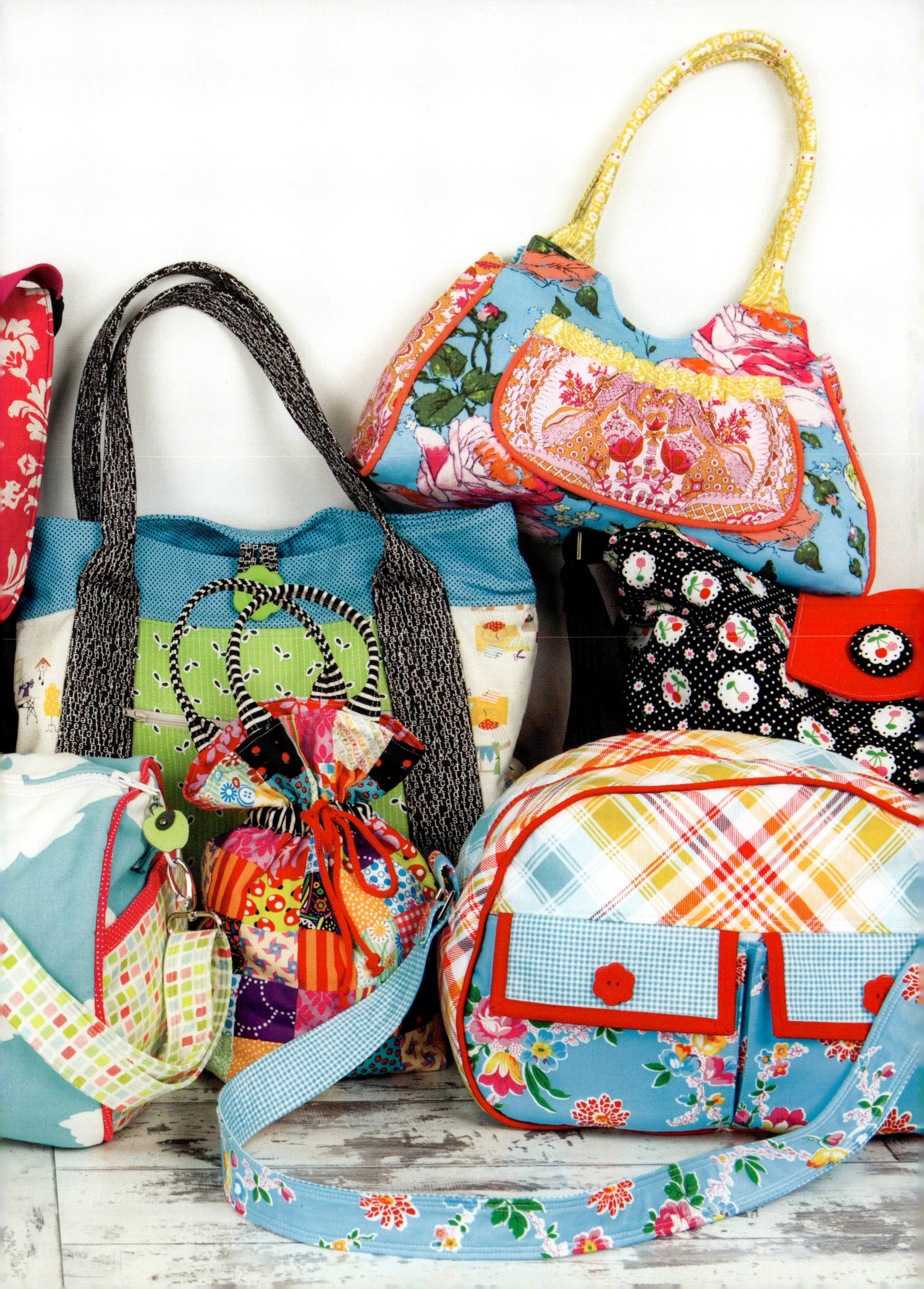

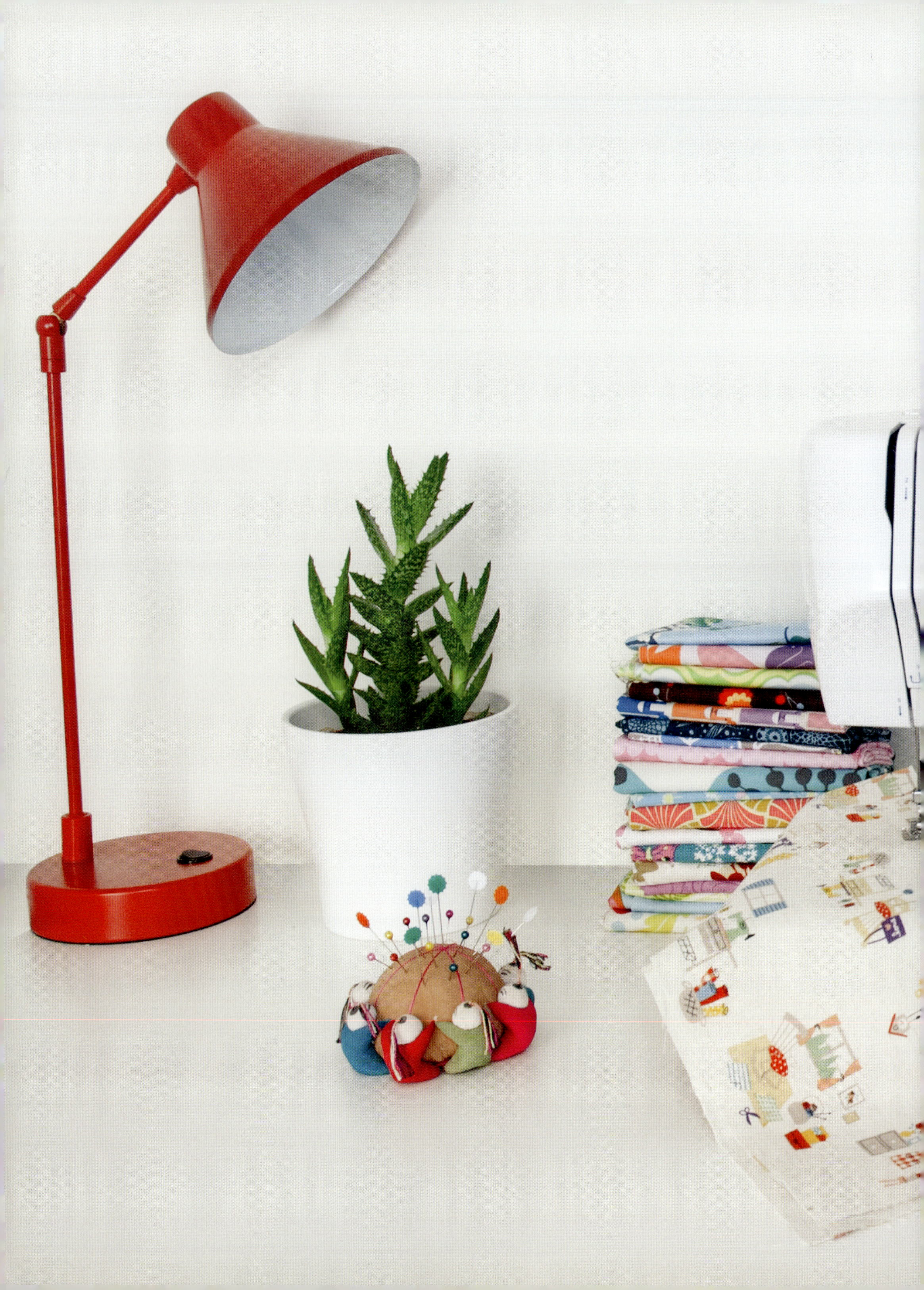

TECHNIQUES

TECHNIQUES

Useful Stitches

The three main stitches used in the projects in this book are topstitch, tacking (basting) and ladder stitch. Here is some useful guidance on how to master these basic stitches.

TOPSTITCH

Topstitch is a line of machine sewing that is used to add a decorative finish and also to attach pockets or other items to your projects.

1. When topstitching for decorative purposes, simply sew a line of normal stitches close to the seam on the right side of your project, as shown. I recommend sewing a distance of 3–5mm (⅛–¼in) away from the seam.

2. When topstitching as a method to attach an element, such as a pocket, to your design simply pin or tack (baste) the item right side up on top of your project (also right side up). Sew the item in place with a line of stitching close to the edge of the item being attached, as shown. I recommend sewing approximately 3mm (⅛in) away from the edge.

① Decorative topstitching 3–5mm (⅛–¼in) away from the seam

② Topstitching to attach a pocket 3mm (⅛in) away from the seam

TACKING (BASTING)

Tacking (basting) is a sewer's best insurance policy! If you want to make sure that your sewing is straight, particularly when stitching fiddly items together, it is a great idea to tack the pieces together before sewing with your machine. Tacking can also give you much greater control and accuracy than simply pinning your items together.

1. To tack two items together, simply place the two pieces together as advised within the sewing instructions, ensuring that they are neatly and evenly positioned. Thread your needle and take medium-to-large running stitches along the seam to be sewn, as shown. You may like to secure with a small knot at the start and end points, depending on the project you are working on.

2. After you have completed your tacking, sew the section with your sewing machine and remove your tacking stitches.

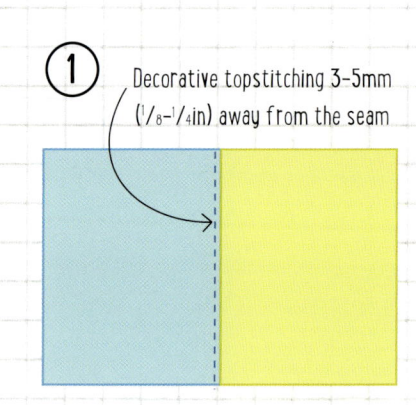

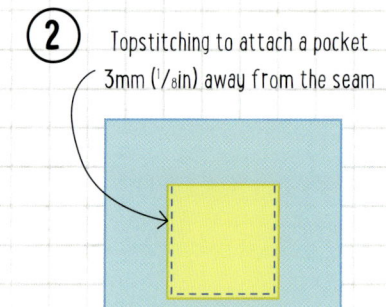

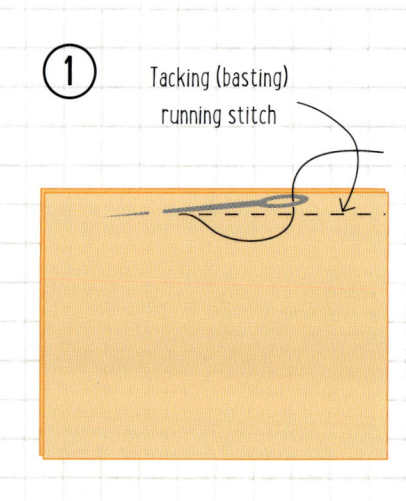

① Tacking (basting) running stitch

LADDER STITCH

Ladder stitch is a fabulous hand stitch that closes seams invisibly. If your prefer, you can quickly topstitch or whip stitch your turning gaps closed, but for a more professional finish I find it worth the effort to master ladder stitch.

1. Position the bag lining right side up so that the turning gap is easily accessible. Make sure that the raw edges of the turning gap section are neatly folded in. If they are a little messy or uneven you may like to press with your finger or an iron, if accessible.

2. Start at one end of the gap, hiding the starting knot on the wrong side. Take a small stitch right along the folded under edge on one side of the gap.

3. Take a second small stitch right along the folded under edge of the other side of the turning gap. This time start the stitch directly in line with where the first stitch exited.

4. Continue taking stitches in the same way, ensuring that you are creating a ladder effect with the thread, as shown. When you have four to five stitches, pull the thread and the two sides of your turning gap will come together neatly.

5. Continue stitching and pulling the thread every four to five stitches until you fully close the gap.

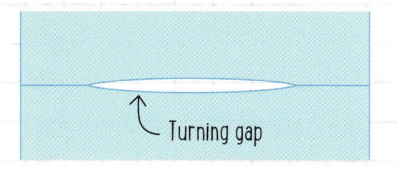

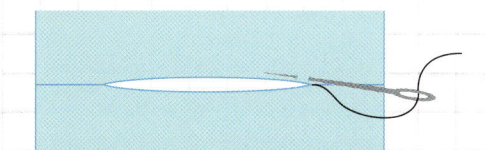

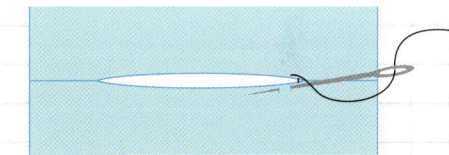

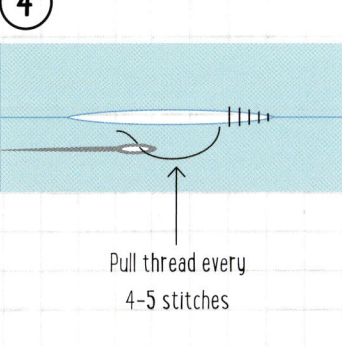

① Bag lining (right side up)

Turning gap

②

③

④

Pull thread every 4-5 stitches

111

Techniques

Creating Piping

Adding piping into seams gives a lovely professional finish to bags and other sewn items. People tend to shy away from using piping as they think it may be difficult or fiddly, but it really is a simple technique and one that is well worth trying out!

1. To make piping you will need a length of fabric that has been cut on the bias. You can either purchase pre-made bias tape and iron out the folds to make a flat straight length of fabric, or cut some of your own fabric on the bias (cut diagonally against the grain of the fabric). As a rule of thumb, you need the width of your unfolded bias strip to measure twice the width of your cord + twice the seam allowance of your project. Therefore, if you are using a 5mm (¼in) cord and a 5mm (¼in) seam allowance, your fabric strip should measure 2.5cm (1in). I like to add a little extra to be on the safe side – you can always trim it later. I would therefore use a 3cm (1¼in) strip in this instance.

2. Lay your cord along the centre of the bias strip. Starting at one end, fold the fabric onto itself, enclosing the cord. Pin in place intermittently.

3. Now attach the zipper foot to your sewing machine and use a thread colour to match the piping fabric. Starting at one end, sew the bias fabric together very close to the piping to fully enclose it all the way along the length. Once fully stitched, your piping is now ready to use in your project.

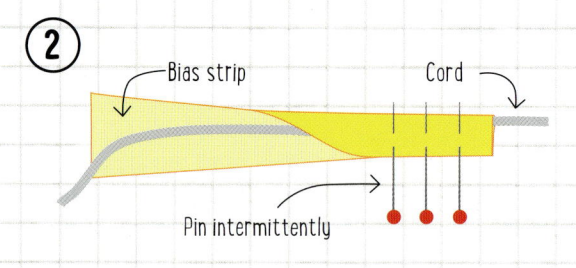

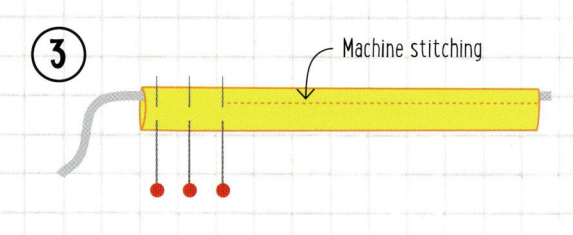

Inserting Magnetic Closures

Magnetic closures are a quick and easy way to make closable openings on your bags or pockets. There is no need to be wary of these, as they are so simple to insert. Unlike some, I like to place magnetic closures into the bag opening as the last step. This ensures they will evenly meet each other after taking into account all the seams and the way the completed bag sits.

1. Take your bag and mark where you want the first side (male side) of the magnetic closure to be inserted on the lining fabric only. To mark this accurately, place the closure washer over the designated location and mark inside the two oval prong holes.

2. Use a seam ripper (quick unpick) to create a small slit along both marked lines. Try to keep the slits smaller than the prongs so that your closure will not be loose on the fabric.

3. Insert the prongs of the male magnetic closure piece through these slits. The prongs will be slightly bigger than the slits, which is intentional – simply push them through for a snug fit. If the piece of fabric you are inserting the closure into already has interfacing, you can now attach the washer over the prongs on the wrong side of the fabric, folding the prongs outwards to enclose the washer and secure the closure. If the fabric does not have interfacing, I recommend that you cut a 4cm (1½in) square of fusible fleece. Fit this over the prongs at the back of your fabric before attaching the washer to give added support, protection and strength.

4. If this is for a bag closure, close the bag so that the front and back top edges are sitting evenly. Now press the male side of the magnetic closure into the other side of the lining, making a slight indent in the fabric where you want the two sides to meet. Using the depression as your placement guide, repeat the Steps 1–3 to install the female side of the closure.

① **Lining fabric (right side)**

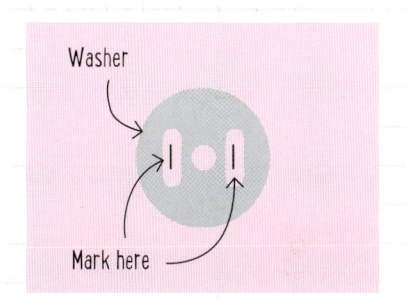

Washer
Mark here

③ **Lining fabric (wrong side)**

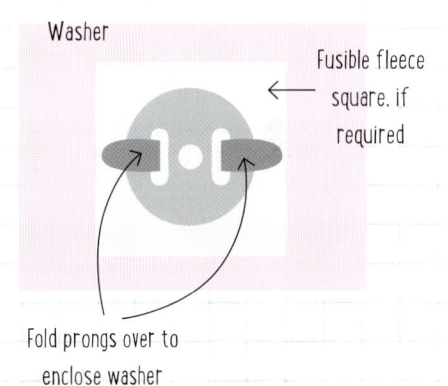

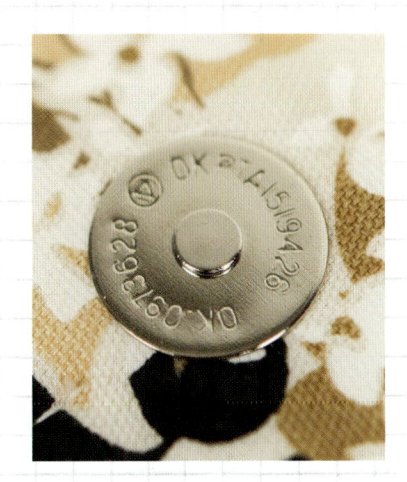

Washer
Fusible fleece square, if required
Fold prongs over to enclose washer

Techniques

Turning Handles

There are two techniques that can be used for turning handles: end gap turning, where you turn from one short end of the handle and middle gap turning, where a gap is left at the centre of one long edge for turning, giving neater handle ends.

END GAP TURNING

Some of the projects in this book will instruct you to sew your handle along three edges, leaving one short end open for turning. You will need a long, thin item, such as a chopstick or paintbrush, to help you with this method.

1. Sew the handle strips together along three edges, as instructed. Snip the corners of the sewn end.

2. Opening and rearranging the handle tube a little to help you, place a long, thin object against the sewn end. Push it though the inside of the handle and out of the open end. For most handles, you will need to gather the handle fabric over your turning object little by little until the end comes through. Then you can manually pull this out the right way.

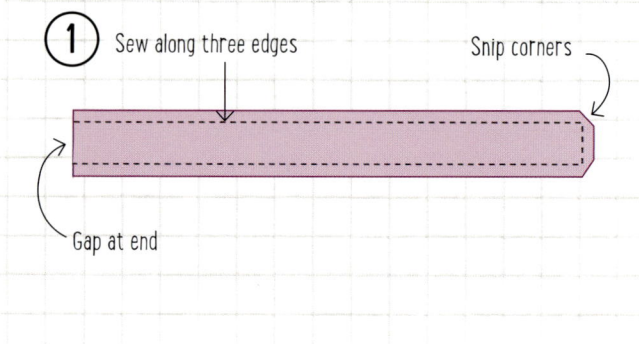

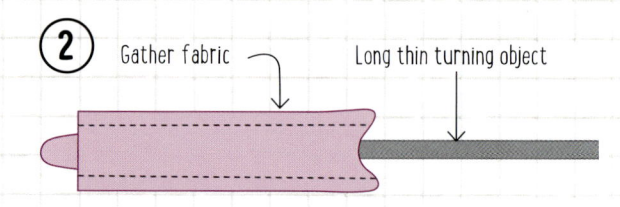

① Sew along three edges — Snip corners — Gap at end

② Gather fabric — Long thin turning object

MIDDLE GAP TURNING.

When the end of a handle is visible it needs to be neatly sewn and turned. In this situation we would leave a turning gap along the middle of one long edge.

1. Sew around all edges of the handle, leaving a gap as instructed. Snip all four corners carefully.

2. Take something long and thin, such as a chopstick or the smooth end of a paintbrush. Opening and rearranging the handle tube a little to help you, push the long object against one of the sewn ends so that it now gets pushed though the inside of the handle and out of the turning gap. For some handles you may need to gather the handle fabric over your turning object little by little until the end comes through. Then you can manually pull it out the right way. Push the corners out fully and neatly before removing the turning tool. Repeat with the other side of the handle.

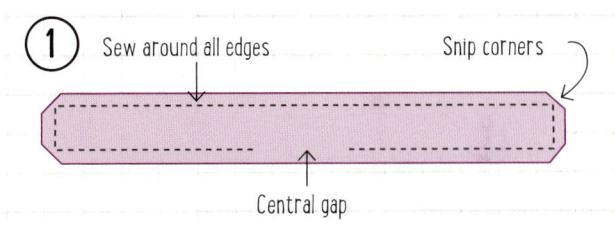

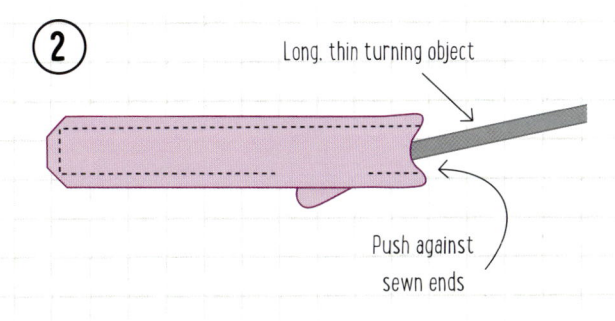

① Sew around all edges — Snip corners — Central gap

② Long, thin turning object — Push against sewn ends

Techniques

Adjustable Straps

When making a larger bag that will be carried with one long shoulder strap, it is a great idea to add the feature of an adjustable strap. This will enable you to shorten and lengthen the strap, making your bag suitable for all different heights and carrying styles!

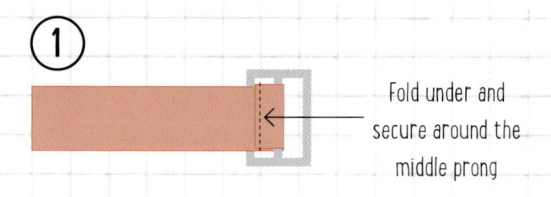

1. Take your completed strap and slide adjuster. Loop one end of the strap around the centre prong in the slide adjuster and fold the strap end onto itself by approximately 2.5cm (1in). Topstitch the fold in place to capture the slide adjuster.

2. Take the remaining free end of the strap. First feed this (from inside to outside) through the ring at one side of the bag. Next fold the strap over, enclosing the ring, and feed the end through the outer two prongs of the slide adjuster, as shown.

3. Take the loose end and thread it (from outside to inside) through the handle ring at the other side of the bag. Fold it under and topstitch the end in place to capture the ring. You can now adjust the strap as desired.

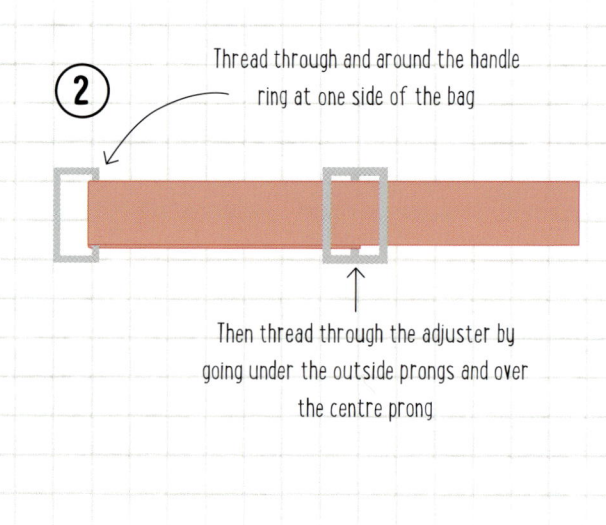

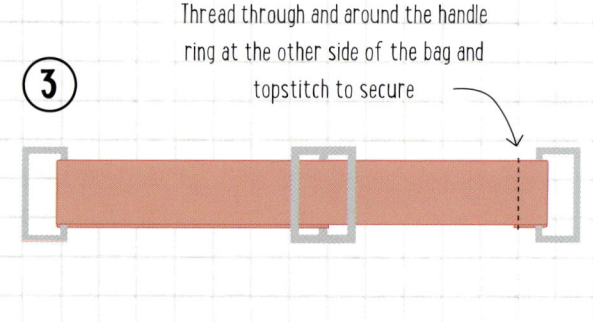

① Fold under and secure around the middle prong

② Thread through and around the handle ring at one side of the bag

Then thread through the adjuster by going under the outside prongs and over the centre prong

③ Thread through and around the handle ring at the other side of the bag and topstitch to secure

Sewing Darts

On some bags you will find a dart marked on the template (see Pattern Pullout Sheet). A dart is a tapered tuck that is sewn into items to give them structure, shape or fullness.

---

1. Take your bag or pocket piece containing the dart.

2. Fold the bag piece, right sides together, so that the raw side edges of the dart triangle are now on top of each other, as shown.

3. Stitch the raw edges together with a sewing machine, tapering the stitches to the folded edge.

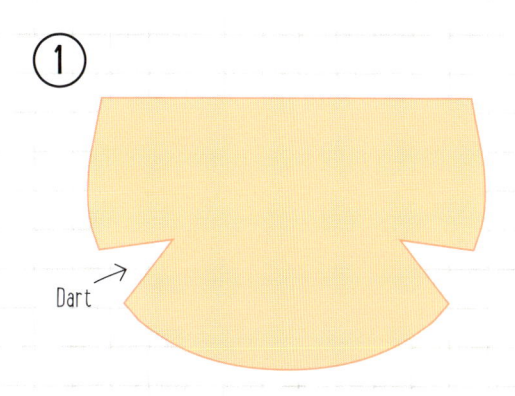

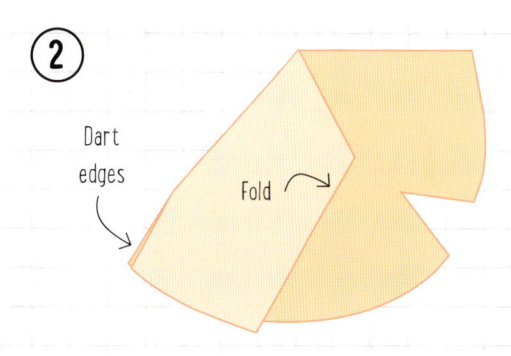

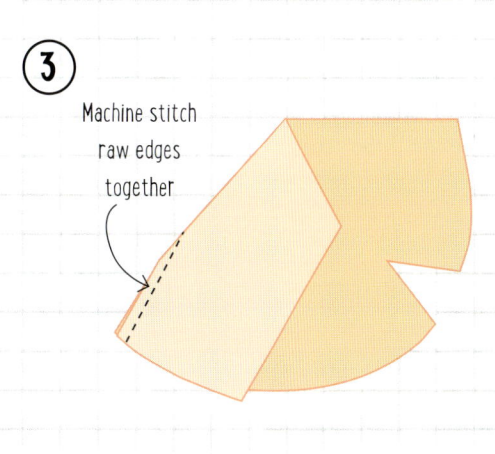

TECHNIQUES

Shortening Zips

I like to always use a longer zip than needed when making bags so that I can shorten them, discarding the messy end pieces. This gives a neat, flat finish to the ends of your zips – it is important to secure the ends when doing this.

1. Sew the fabric pieces to your zip as instructed in the pattern, so that it is as shown.

2. It is important that you now open the zip a little so that the zip pull is within the fabric section of your work. Using your sewing machine, or by hand, sew backwards and forwards over the teeth of the zip, approximately 3mm (⅛in) inside the edges of your work. These stitches will act much like the metal stoppers at the ends of the zip until the bag is fully constructed.

3. You can now safely trim off the ends of your zip, in line with the sides of your fabric.

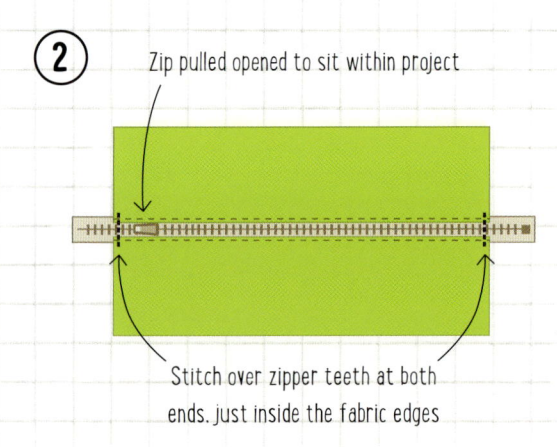

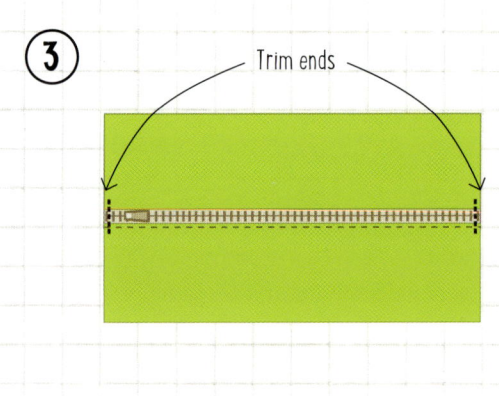

①

② Zip pulled opened to sit within project

Stitch over zipper teeth at both ends, just inside the fabric edges

③ Trim ends

118

Topstitch Binding

It is easy to neaten pocket edges with a touch of added flair by adding a line of binding to a raw edge. It makes a good design feature and adds strength to the edges. I choose to attach topstitch binding, firstly because I like its appearance and secondly it is a much quicker and easier way to add traditional continuous binding.

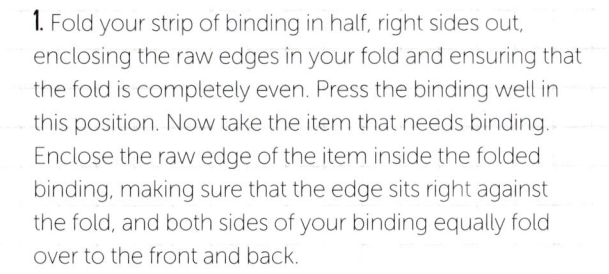

1. Fold your strip of binding in half, right sides out, enclosing the raw edges in your fold and ensuring that the fold is completely even. Press the binding well in this position. Now take the item that needs binding. Enclose the raw edge of the item inside the folded binding, making sure that the edge sits right against the fold, and both sides of your binding equally fold over to the front and back.

2. Tack (baste) or pin the binding in position, making sure that it equally covers the front and back edges. Then sew in place approximately 3mm (⅛in) from the inner edge.

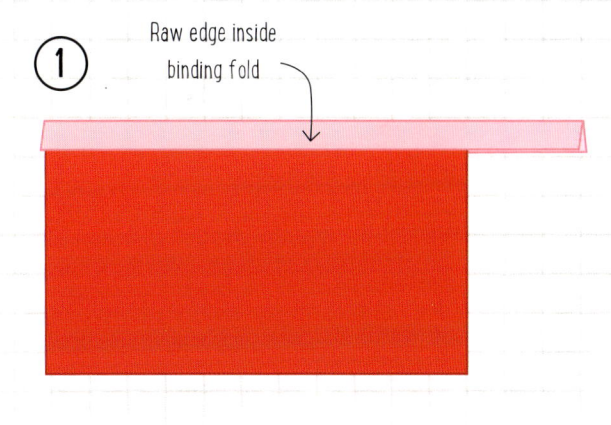

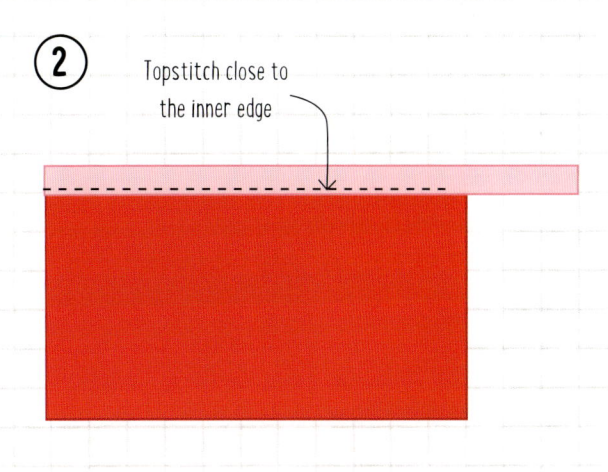

TECHNIQUES

Mitred Corners

When binding the edges of a project, you will usually come across some corners. The neatest way to bind your corners is to mitre them. In this book I have used two different methods of binding: standard continuous binding, as used for City Nights Clutch and mitred topstitch binding, as used for Mobile Mummy Changing Bag and Sugar Sweet Shoulder Bag.

STANDARD CONTINUOUS BINDING

When using continuous binding you will need to machine stitch the binding to the front of your bag using a method that creates the front mitre folds and allows the back mitre fold to be made during hand sewing.

1. Sew the raw edges of the binding in place on your project, right sides together. When you come across your first corner, sew until you are the seam allowance distance away from the edge and secure your stitching at this point.

2. Fold the unsewn binding up and away from your item, so that the raw edge is now in line with the angle of the next edge to be bound.

3. Fold the binding back down to lay against the raw edge. Start sewing at the same (seam allowance) distance from the corner.

4. Now the binding is mitred from the front. Later you will fold the binding over to the wrong side and ladder stitch it in place (see Useful Stitches). When you reach the corners, simply fold them into neat mitres at the front and back as you sew that section. As a result of the machine stitching they will almost form themselves with a little adjusting and folding.

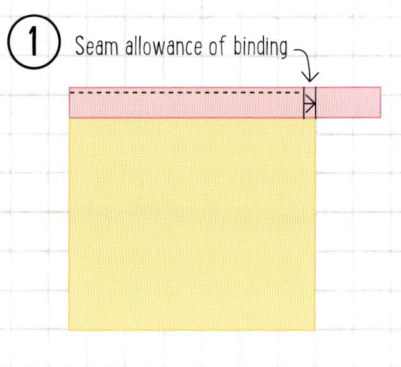

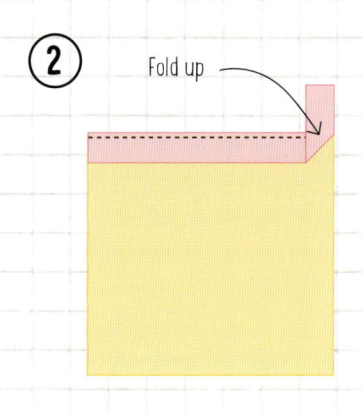

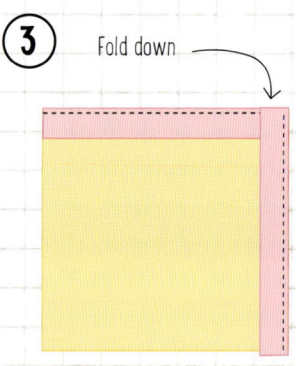

① Seam allowance of binding

② Fold up

③ Fold down

MITRED TOPSTITCH BINDING

When topstitching your binding in place, you are sewing the front and back of your binding at once. Therefore we must use a method to fold and create the mitres on both sides, before topstitching them into position.

1. Fit the binding over the edge of the item to be bound so that the raw edge of the item fits inside and against the fold in the binding. Topstitch in place close to the inner edge, all the way to the first corner.

2. Remove from your sewing machine. Fold the binding down to the second edge, matching the fold in the binding up with the raw edge again. This naturally creates a triangle that you will need to fold over to the front edge to make your mitre. You may need to rearrange and neaten as you go.

3. Fold the other side of the binding to the back in the same way. Making sure that both sides are even, pin or tack (baste) in place, then continue the topstitching, starting right at the mitre to secure.

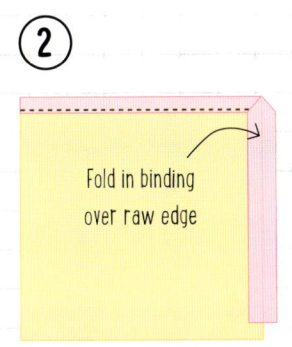

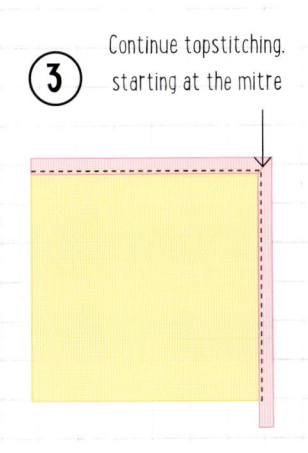

① Topstitch to first corner

② Fold in binding over raw edge

③ Continue topstitching, starting at the mitre

Techniques

Box Corners

If you were to simply sew two squares of fabric together, you would create a very flat bag. While this is great for a gift bag, book bag or simple tote, sometimes you may like your bag to be more three-dimensional and have added depth to hold more inside. In these cases we often use box corners. In my patterns there are two different types of box corners: square edge box corners, as used in Melly's Messenger and Luscious Layered Bag and cut out box corners, as used in Mobile Mummy Changing Bag and Wine and Dine Duo.

SQUARE EDGE BOX CORNERS

This form of box corners is the most common method used in bag patterns. Simply create your bag as usual, then add depth by sewing across the corners at different widths, depending on your desired depth.

1. Once you have sewn the bag front and back together you will have two squared off bottom corners, as shown.

2. Keeping the main bag inside out, open up the bag and re-fold it to position the side sewn seam on top of the bottom sewn seam, right sides together. This will create a triangle with its peak being the bottom corner of the bag, as shown.

3. Mark and then sew across the end of the triangle where it measures the specified width. For example, the following diagram demonstrates an instruction to mark and sew where the triangle measures 5cm (2in).

4. Cut the excess fabric at the triangle peak away, approximately 5mm (¼in) outside of the sewn line.

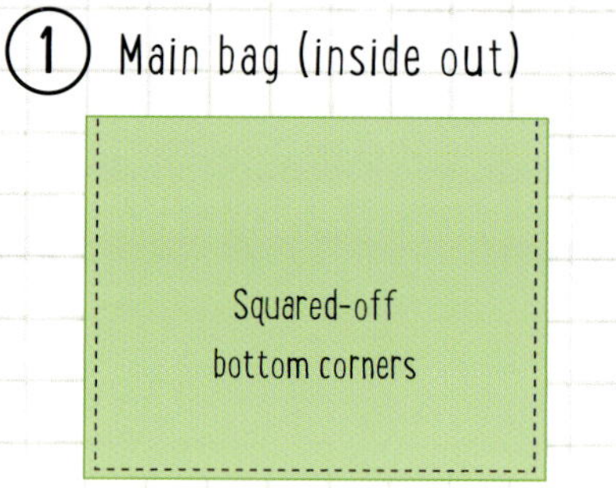

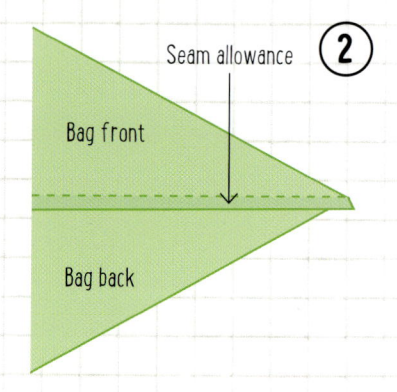

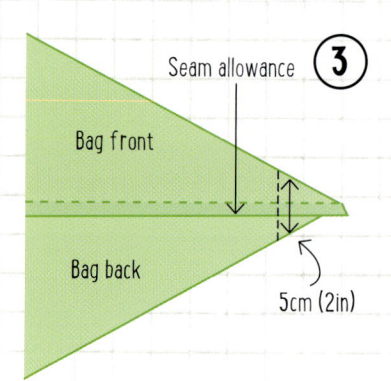

① Main bag (inside out)

Squared-off bottom corners

② Seam allowance

Bag front

Bag back

③ Seam allowance

Bag front

Bag back

5cm (2in)

CUT-OUT BOX CORNERS

Cut-out box corners are ideal if you need to add something into the seam, such as with the Mobile Mummy Changing Bag. They also make it easier to achieve a very square bottom with less piecing and wastage, as with the Wine and Dine Duo.

1. Once you have sewn the bag front and back together along the side and bottom edges, you will have two remaining cut out bottom corners, as shown.

2. Keeping the main bag inside out, open up the bag and re-fold it to position the side sewn seam on top of the bottom sewn seam, right sides together. This will create a trapezoid with the top raw edges being the bottom cut out corner of the bag, as shown.

3. Making sure that the raw edges and seams meet evenly, simply sew across with a 5mm (¼in) seam allowance to create your box corner.

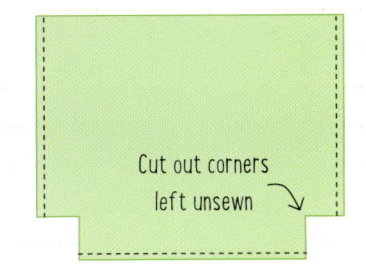

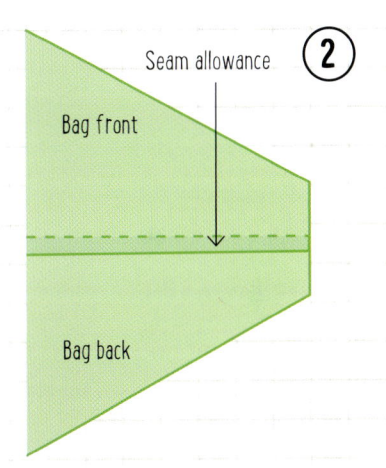

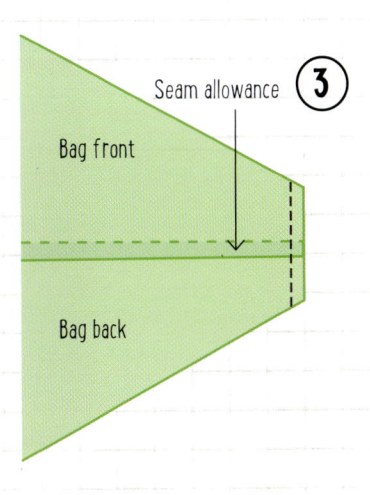

① Main bag (inside out)

Cut out corners left unsewn

② Seam allowance

Bag front

Bag back

③ Seam allowance

Bag front

Bag back

SUPPLIERS

AUSTRALIA

Melly & me
www.mellyandme.com

Creative Abundance
www.creativeabundance.com.au

Fabric Patch
www.fabricpatch.com.au

Patchwork with Gail B
www.patchworkwithgailb.com

Spotlight
www.spotlight.com.au

The Oz Material Girls
www.theozmaterialgirls.com

Under the Mulberry Tree
www.underthemulberrytree.com

VooDoo Rabbit
www.voodoorabbit.com.au

UK

Cross Patch
www.cross-patch.co.uk

Hulu Crafts
www.hulucrafts.co.uk

Prints to Polka Dots
www.printstopolkadots.co.uk

The Fat Quarters
www.thefatquarters.co.uk

Stitch Craft Create
www.stitchcraftcreate.co.uk

USA

Heartsong Quilts
www.heartsongquilts.com

Pine Needles
www.pineneedlesonline.com

Pink Chalk Fabrics
www.pinkchalkfabrics.com

Martha Pullen
www.marthapullen.com

CANADA

Emmaline
www.emmalinebags.com

The Nuts for Bolts, Etc.
www.nutsforboltsetc.com

THANK YOU!

Firstly, I would like to thank each and every one of you who has purchased this book and who have been a part of my Melly & Me journey so far. I continually feel so blessed to be able to live this creative life and share my creativity with so many gorgeous like-minded sewers.

Thank you to all at David & Charles for allowing me to bring another stunning book into reality. You are always such a pleasure to work with!

I wish to thank my fabulous team of test sewers who were so enthusiastic and encouraging, giving me great feedback about their sewing experiences when testing the bags. You girls are such a crucial part of the process and I couldn't have done it without you!

And last but by far not least, I wish to thank my delicious family who always support and encourage me to follow my creative dreams. Thank you for listening to my overexcited – and at times stressed out – ramblings and for always telling me that I can do it, no matter what my dreams are.

THE AUTHOR

Melanie McNeice is an Aussie pattern designer, based in the leafy outskirts of Melbourne, Australia. Melly's adventures in sewing were born only nine years ago, after she found herself a stay at home mum with the desire to still be productive. Her passion for sewing grew quickly after her sister encouraged her to give it a try, and only twelve months after beginning to sew, she tried her hand at design under the pattern label 'Melly & Me'.

Melly's goals in design are to create a range of contemporary sewing patterns that include bright and quirky toys and wearable purses, as well as fun and modern quilts. Melanie aims to design items that are original and fun, achievable in a day, as well as being completely useable in everyday life!

Since its beginnings, Melly & Me has grown to appeal to a worldwide audience. Melly has designed in excess of 90 patterns, published her first three books, *Kaleidoscope*, *Sewn Toy Tales* and *Snug as a Bug*, and teaches across Australia. In 2010, Melly also began her journey in fabric design having released five fabric collections since that time.

Melly takes inspiration from her two young children, childhood memories and the beauty of nature, as well as her love of fun and colour!

Visit Melly's website to see more of her fun designs at www.mellyandme.com.

Backpack, Blue Skies 38–45
basting (tacking) 110
Beautiful Blooms Handbag 18–23
bias tape 12, 66
bias tape markers 12
binding 28–9, 78, 102–3
    mitre topstitch 78, 121
    standard continuous 29, 120
    topstitch 28, 78, 102, 119
Blue Skies Backpack 38–45
book bags 52
bottle bags 82–7
box corners 36–7, 50, 52, 65, 87–8, 94, 96, 122–3
    cut out box 123
    square edge 122
buckles 49–51, 52
button closure strips 37, 58–9
buttons 73
    self cover 12, 63, 66, 93, 96

Carry-All, Cute 30–7
Changing Bag, Mobile Mummy 60–7
changing mats 66
chequerboard designs 82–9
City Nights Clutch 24–9
closures
    button closure strips 37, 58–9
    buttons 12, 73
    magnetic 14, 23, 41, 52, 59, 73, 78–9, 113
    Velcro 64, 66
    zips 14, 34, 42, 80, 102, 104–5, 118
Clutch, City Nights 24–9
cord 12
corners
    mitred 66, 78, 120–1
    see also box corners
cotton 12
Cute Carry-All 30–7

elastic 22

fabric 12
    scraps 85
fabric markers 10
fusible fleece/interfacing 12

gathers 22
gusset rings 80

Handbag, Beautiful Blooms 18–23

handle rings 14, 65–6, 80, 95
handles 23, 35, 57, 59, 77, 80, 85, 87–8, 93, 105
    end gap turning 114
    interfaced 21, 33, 85, 93, 101
    middle gap turning 115
    turning 23, 35, 43, 80, 86–8, 96, 105, 114–15
Happy Hobo Bag 54–9

ladder stitch 111
lunch bags 82–9
Luscious Layered Bag 90–7

magnetic closures 14, 23, 41, 52, 59, 73, 78–9, 113
materials 12
Melly's Messenger 46–53
mitred corners 66, 78, 120–1
Mobile Mummy Changing Bag 60–7

needles
    hand sewing 10
    sewing machine 10

overnight bags 98–105

patchwork 27
piping 21–4, 77, 79, 101, 104, 112
pleats 64
pockets 21–3, 36, 41–2, 49, 51, 57–9, 63–5, 77–9, 102–3

ring holders 43, 77, 79–80, 102, 103
ring loops 95–6
rings 14, 65–6, 80, 95, 103
rotary cutters 10
Ruffle Duffle 98–105
ruffles 94–6, 102–3

scissors 10
sewing darts 28–9, 42, 58–9, 117
Shopaholics Shopper 68–73
slide adjusters 14, 66
sports bags 98–105
stitch directory 110–11
strap adjusters 14, 44, 66
straps 43–4, 51–2
    adjustable 66, 105, 116
    interfaced 101
    ring pieces 103
Sugar Sweet Shoulder Bag 74–81

swivel hooks 14

tacking (basting) 110
template plastic 10
thread 10
ties 66
tools
    bag making 12–14
    basic sewing kit 10
topstitch 110
tracing paper 10

Velcro 64, 66

webbing 12
Wine & Dine Duo 82–9

zipper feet 14
zipper pulls 14
zips 14, 34, 42, 80, 102, 104–5
    shortening 118

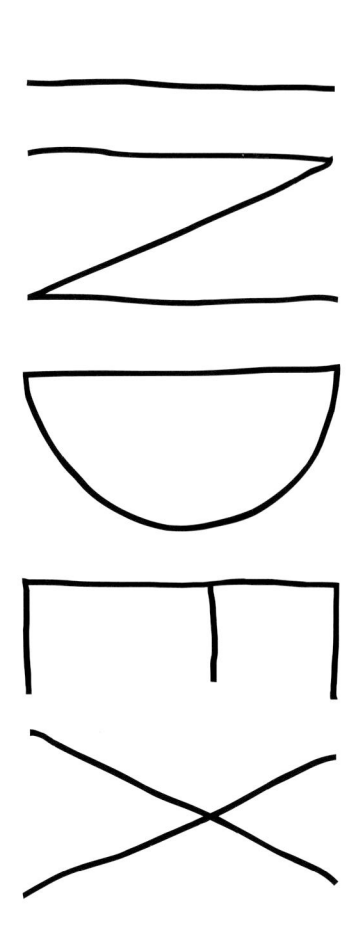

A DAVID & CHARLES BOOK
© F&W Media International, Ltd 2014

David & Charles is an imprint of F&W Media International, Ltd
Brunel House, Forde Close, Newton Abbot, TQ12 4PU, UK

F&W Media International, Ltd is a subsidiary of F+W Media, Inc
10151 Carver Road, Suite #200, Blue Ash, OH 45242, USA

Text and Designs © Melly McNeice 2014

Layout and Photography © F&W Media International, Ltd 2014

First published in the UK and USA in 2014

Melly McNeice has asserted her right to be identified as author of this work in accordance with the Copyright, Designs and Patents Act, 1988.

All rights reserved. No part of this publication may be reproduced in any form or by any means, electronic or mechanical, by photocopying, recording or otherwise, without prior permission in writing from the publisher.

Readers are permitted to reproduce any of the patterns or designs in this book for their personal use and without the prior permission of the publisher. However, the designs in this book are copyright and must not be reproduced for resale.

The author and publisher have made every effort to ensure that all the instructions in the book are accurate and safe, and therefore cannot accept liability for any resulting injury, damage or loss to persons or property, however it may arise.

Names of manufacturers and product ranges are provided for the information of readers, with no intention to infringe copyright or trademarks.

A catalogue record for this book is available from the British Library.

ISBN-13: 978-1-4463-0418-1 paperback
ISBN-10: 1-4463-0418-3 paperback

Printed in China by RR Donnelley for:
F&W Media International, Ltd
Brunel House, Forde Close, Newton Abbot, TQ12 4PU, UK

10 9 8 7 6 5 4 3 2 1

Acquisitions Editor: Sarah Callard
Desk Editor: Harriet Butt
Project Editor: Beth Dymond
Art Editor: Anna Fazakerley
Photographer: Jack Gorman
Production Controller: Kelly Smith

F+W Media publishes high quality books on a wide range of subjects.
For more great book ideas visit: www.stitchcraftcreate.co.uk